What people ar

101 Winning Marketing Actions for Small Businesses

"In her book, *101 Winning Marketing Actions for Small Businesses*, Janet Christy provides a comprehensive, action-based approach for small business owners. Effective marketing is a cornerstone for any business. This book gives 101 specific action steps to take toward successful marketing and includes plenty of room for planning, jotting notes and keeping track of progress. As the co-owner of a small, woman-owned marketing business, I believe the information in *101 Winning Marketing Actions* will be helpful to those just starting out as well as veterans who've been in their respective fields for years. As a marketing professional, I found numerous informational gems that will be useful to me!

Jill Pertler

Co-owner, Marketing by Design; Syndicated columnist, "Slices of Life"

Author of "The Do-It-Yourselfer's Guide to Self-Syndication"

101 Winning Marketing Actions for Small Businesses

A Workshop in a Book for
Small, Woman-Owned, Minority-Owned and Disadvantaged Businesses

Janet W. Christy

BookLocker

Bangor, Maine

BookLocker

P O Box 2399

Bangor, ME 04402-2399

www.booklocker.com

ACKNOWLEDGEMENTS

Thank you to the Small Business Owners who took the time to provide feedback on this book during its development. Special thanks to: Beverly Deal, Bernell King Ingram, Susan Linsley, Patti Madden, Lori Morton, Raquel Rowe and June Wilcox.

I am very grateful to Karen Collier for her help in editing, proofing and keeping the book practical.

Thanks to Sharon Free, the Creative Diva, for designing the terrific cover of this book.

A special thanks to my parents, Charles and Marion Whiting, for helping me understand the importance of two well-known sayings:

- If it's worth doing, it's worth doing right
- Be kind to and respectful of other people

TABLE OF CONTENTS

INTRODUCTION

Have you ever said or thought any of the following:

o Could I get that coffee straight into my vein, please?
o I need to lose five pounds by this weekend.
o Call me back right away!
o That hostess thinks I'm gonna wait 20 minutes for a table, are you kidding?
o If you are going to drive the speed limit then get in the right lane!

Today it seems that we not only want instant results, but we often feel it is our right to expect and receive things immediately. We always have what we think are good reasons to justify this need for immediacy. Some of those reasons appear in the rationalization Small Business Owners use to explain why they haphazardly market their business and why they do little, if any, Marketing Planning and Research.

Have you ever used any of the following justifications?

o Why make a Marketing Plan, the marketplace drives my Customers.
o I'm too busy servicing my Customers to market my business.
o I don't have time to do research.
o I'd like to get some government business, but I don't know how (*or* it's too complicated).
o I have a Marketing Plan – call on 30 people every week.

In your hands you now have a "workshop in a book" that provides you 101 Actions that yield immediate results and collectively produce a marketing action plan.

When I was in telecommunications marketing/sales we Account Managers were required to develop and use Marketing Action Plans – MAPs. In developing these MAPs (plans) we listed Actions, established time frames for them and identified roles and responsibilities for carrying out the Actions. Some of the marketing research was done for us because we had assigned geographic territories and customer types such as: Professional Services, Medical, Government, Manufacturing, etc. When I first worked in telecommunications we operated as a utility so we were to market/sell to everyone in our assigned area and business type. However, after we really had competition, management realized we needed to operate more like a business than a utility and Account Managers were instructed to incorporate qualification of prospects into our MAPs (plans).

Most businesses, whether large or small, that are successful have some type of Marketing Plan that includes activities with time-frames. So if you are operating without a Marketing Plan or have one but it needs updating or is not helping, you can increase your success by following the Actions in this book.

The book provides 101 Marketing Actions that, when used, provide you understanding, activities, templates, methods and challenges. These Actions will simplify your marketing and sales efforts and make them more efficient and productive. If you use the Actions and set time-frames for them you will have a Marketing Action Plan – MAP. Many of the Actions utilize forms and examples to help you understand and get started. There are even some Actions that give you immediate payback.

All the Actions may not apply to your business or they may not be feasible now. In the last Chapter of the book (Chapter 9) is a list of all the Actions with a place for you to make notes or set dates for future use or consideration.

Some concepts that you will see throughout the Actions are:

- o Subcontracting – an approach that increases your opportunities by allowing you to participate in the big projects.
- o Outsourcing – being the recipient of outsourced projects, processes and functions
- o Partnering – another method for increasing your opportunities.
- o Focused – meaning alert, targeted and homed-in; all things that will make your Marketing Actions simpler and more productive.
- o Doing – the book uses Actions instead of Tips because Actions will move you forward and get results for your business.

Some of the Actions are dependent on or intertwined with others, but most of them do not have to be done in a specific order. The Actions are divided into 8 sections to help you choose the ones that apply to your specific situation at a specific time. A chapter is devoted to each section:

- Chapter 1 – BEGINNING
- Chapter 2 – PHILOSOPHY
- Chapter 3 – PREPARATION
- Chapter 4 – PROSPECTING
- Chapter 5 – GETTING THE WORD OUT / GETTING NOTICED
- Chapter 6 – TRADE FAIRS & NETWORKING
- Chapter 7 – FOLLOW UP / FOLLOW THROUGH
- Chapter 8 -- SCHEDULE

Chapter 1
<u>BEGINNING</u>

Action #1

<u>Learn and understand these acronyms and words.</u>

These terms are important because they help you be prepared to see and act on opportunities that are geared or directed toward your specific business type. Committing these terms to memory will make you more aware and vigilant. Before electronic games and DVD players in cars, children played games on a trip such as counting cars of a specific color. Say your car color to count was red and your brother's color was blue. You would notice every red car passing, in parking lots, in front or in back of you. That is the way it should be with these acronyms; just as if you were competing against your sibling, you are competing against other businesses and you need to notice the opportunities.

- Small Business = the SBA (Small Business Administration) publishes a guide to determine if your business is officially a Small Business. The table can be found at: http://www.sba.gov/idc/groups/public/documents/sba_homep age/serv_sstd_tablepdf.pdf.
  You may be surprised what is considered "small."
- WBE = Woman Business Enterprise
- MBE = Minority Business Enterprise (may include non-minority women)
- M/WBE = Minority/Woman Business Enterprise
- W/MBE = Woman/Minority Business Enterprise

- HUB = Historically Underutilized Business (includes minorities and usually includes non-minority women)
- VOSB = Veteran Owned Small Business
- SDVOSB = Service Disabled Veteran Owned Small Business
- Disadvantaged Business = a business that is disadvantaged because of its size, owners gender or race, lack of opportunity in its location and some other less defined factors
- Diverse Suppliers/Vendors = any of the above qualify.

Keep these acronyms handy because you will see them throughout this book.

Action #2

<u>Be sure your Prospects, Customers and Clients understand what your Products and Services are.</u>

Have you ever had someone ask if you offer a particular product or service and you cannot understand how they could possibly have thought that it was related to your business? Before you assume it was their fault, step back and take a look at your marketing messages and activities. Are your messages clear? Are you trying to be/offer too much and confusing people?

Guard against grouping things together that are not easily seen as related. If you do coaching and sell nutritional products, treat them as separate businesses and don't mix them in your materials, websites, etc. If you offer too many products/services or things that are very different it can make you look as if you are not good enough at something specific.

Remember that it is not enough for you to understand your message – the recipient of your message needs to understand it.

Action #3

If your objective is to help people, start or join a non-profit organization.

If you have a business or are thinking about starting one make sure that you can distinguish between a business and a non-profit. If your primary intent is to "help" people then you may not have a business or business idea. If your intent is to make money, then you have a business or business idea. Now, you can certainly make money by helping people. But if revenue is the byproduct and a "cause" is the main reason for your effort then you should probably start or become a non-profit.

If you really want to make money, but you are uncomfortable with that way of thinking you have some soul searching to do. You will have to address your discomfort and give yourself permission to be successful at making money if you are to succeed as a business.

Some other factors that may steer you toward a non-profit instead of a business are:
- Your Prospects need your services but cannot pay for them
- You need to pursue grant funding to operate
- The product/service you offer (or want to offer) is considered charity or altruistic
- You want to change something such as a policy, a law or a social prejudice

Action #4

Know and respect your competition.

If you do not know your competition or you ignore them you are living dangerously!

This book includes many Actions that lead you to meetings, conferences, websites, situations and activities that your competition may already be utilizing. These things offer you excellent opportunities to observe and learn about your competition. Pair this observation with a little research on their website and you will see what they do and how they do it. You can discover how they market their products/services and what advantages or weaknesses they have. This knowledge will prepare you to more effectively compete and win.

The knowledge will also help you find partners in businesses that you would normally have seen only as a competitor. When you understand what they do/offer and what they don't do/offer you may find that they actually compliment your business in some situations. That's called co-opetition. Just be sure you establish a written agreement (see page 74 for guidance).

Action #5

Accept the fact that registration with Prospects is an essential step in the marketing process, but is not the last step. Prepare yourself to register.

Most government entities, schools and corporations require that you be registered in their database as a vendor or supplier. It **is** a requirement, many times even part of a "qualification test," but it simply means you are on the list. You still need to market your business to the User of your products and services. Many of the Actions in this book are things you can do to effectively market your business using the angle of being a Small, Disadvantaged or

Minority/Woman/Veteran Owned Business, but do not skip this crucial first step. Think of it as free advertising.

More and more purchasers are using online registration for their database. Listed here are the typical pieces of information that are requested in an online vendor registration. Use the following list as a guide to begin gathering information. Each online registration form will have its own format and, likely, will request something you think is irrelevant. So remember that the form is designed to meet the potential Customer's/Client's needs and the "customer is always right."

The typical information required in an online vendor registration:

- Company Name
- Company Structure (Sole Proprietorship, LLC, etc.)
- Contact Name, Phone and Email
- Website
- Number of employees
- Capabilities/Type (manufacturing, service, distribution, etc.) – there is often a drop down box of choices
- Geographic areas you can serve
- Dun & Bradstreet Number (D&B) or DUNS Number*
- Federal Tax Number (FEIN or Social Security)*
- Date company established
- Last year's annual revenue
- Parent company (if applicable)
- Products and Services – a drop down box with a list of choices may be supplied
- NAICS and/or SIC Codes, NIGP Codes if government *
- References including contact information (be sure the reference is relevant to the government, education, business whose database you are registering on and that you have permission to include them)
- Small Business/Diversity Category (Small, Woman/Minority/Veteran Owned, Disadvantaged, etc. – a drop down box of choices will probably be supplied)

- Documentation of Diversity Certification (you will likely need to upload this so be sure you have scanned the certificate if you did not receive an electronic copy)

* Additional information on these terms is included in this chapter.

Action #6

Obtain a Federal Tax ID Number.

This is also known as FEIN and EIN (Employer Identification Number). It is used to identify a business entity. Businesses generally need the number, according to the IRS website (http://www.irs.gov/businesses/small/article/0,,id=98350,00.html). If you do business with the Federal Government, any Federal Prime Contractors and most other government entities or large businesses, you will need this number. If you are a sole proprietor you may be able to use your Social Security Number. (Note: Using a Social Security Number as the tax identification for your business is a security risk because your SS Number is more available for identity theft). The Federal Tax ID number or a Social Security Number is required to register on CCR (Central Contractor Registration), which is discussed in a later Action on page 106. The above listed website will help you determine if you do need an EIN. Even if you are not required to use an EIN you may want to anyway because it is one of those little things that enhance the professional look of your business. You can apply for this number online, by phone, email or fax and it only takes a few minutes. It will take between 2 to 5 weeks for your EIN to become active; so it is important to do this in time to have it active before you need to use it.

Make record of this number in a secure place.

Note: The IRS does not charge for this service. If you do not use the IRS website or forms to apply you could be charged.

Action #7

Determine the SCI and NAICS Codes that apply to your business.

SIC (Standard Industrial Classification) and NAICS (North American Industry Classification System) are codes that identify and classify your business type. NAICS is the newer and expanded system; it is the most common, but some still use SICs. These codes are used by many businesses and government entities to identify vendors by product/service. You are often asked to register as a vendor with a business or government agency and in that registration include SIC and/or NAICS codes. It is very important to use the correct codes and to use the type of code (SIC or NAICS) that is preferred by your Prospect. You can determine your NAICS codes at www.naics.com/search.htm. This same website will allow you to determine which SIC codes apply to your business after you determine your NAICS codes. If you have already determined your codes, take a look at the list to be sure you don't need to add or delete some. You should do this editing whenever you add or eliminate products/services, but be sure you do it at least once a year.

List your NAICS and SIC Codes here for future reference:

NAICS	SIC	Description

Note: *If you plan to sell your products and services to cities, counties and school districts you will need to take the following* ***Action.***

Action #8

Determine the NIGP Codes that apply to and identify your business products and services to local government agencies.

NIGP is the National Institute of Governmental Purchasing www.nigp.org. This organization provides support and training for governmental purchasers/buyers. The organization has developed a list of codes to assist government purchasers/buyers in automating purchasing. Cities, counties, school districts and some state government agencies are the most likely users of these codes.

These codes are required by many government entities of any business that wants to be placed on their vendor/bidder list. Many government entities list the codes on their websites or in their purchasing information. It is important to spend time looking through the very long list and choosing the ones that best apply to your business, because this is what will be used to identify you as a possible vendor or bidder. If a government agency uses an automated vendor database and they search by NIGP Code for vendors that supply a specific product or service you need to be registered in their database with that Code. Getting it wrong will result in missed opportunities. Keep a record of the codes you choose, so you do not have to look them up every time you need them. If you have already determined your codes, take a look at the list to be sure you don't need to add or delete some. You should do this editing whenever you add or eliminate products/services, but at least once a year.

Note: NIGP uses the term "Commodity" instead or product or service.

You can subscribe to online access to the current codes and all updates from the NIGP or you can look at the purchasing website for a city, county or school district near you. You should revisit the list at least once a year to be sure you are claiming all the NIGP Codes that apply to you.

List your NIGP Codes here so that you have them handy.

NIGP Code	Description

Action #9

Obtain DUNS Number

DUNS (Data Universal Numbering System) numbers are provided by Dun & Bradstreet (D&B). It is an identification number unique to your business or business location. This number is required to register on CCR the Federal Central Contractor Registration (see Action on page 106). Commercial businesses and Federal Prime Contractors also use it to learn more about your business.

You can register at http://fedgov.dnb.com/webform/displayHomePage.do. There is no charge if you request your DUNS number at this website. You will likely be contacted by D&B sales people about additional services that have fees after you register; you will need to assess your personal business situation to determine if these additional services would be beneficial.

Make note of your DUNS here and with your FEIN Number for future reference _____.

Action #10

Determine if one or more Certifications would be advantageous to your business.

There is not a Certification for being a Small Business, but there are qualifications as established by the Small Business Administration (SBA). You can determine if your business meets the qualifications at http://web.sba.gov/faqs/faqindex.cfm?areaID=15.

Being certified as a Minority-Owned, Woman-Owned, Veteran-Owned or Disadvantaged Business is not beneficial for everyone, but for some businesses it can be an advantage. To better understand Certification let's look at some definitions for the word certify:

1. Attest as certain; confirm
2. Guarantee; endorse reliability
3. Award a certificate attesting to the passing of a qualifying examination
4. Give assurance; testify; vouch for the validity of something

All of these definitions apply to the Certification of a business being Minority/Woman/Veteran Owned or Disadvantaged.

When you apply for a Certification you, the business owner(s), are asking an organization or government agency to guarantee that you meet <u>all</u> their qualifications for being endorsed as Minority-Owned, Woman-Owned, Veteran-Owned or Disadvantaged You are asking that organization/agency to provide you a certificate attesting that you meet the qualifications. The reputation of that organization/agency is on the line when they certify you, so they will look closely at your credentials, records and claims. If they erroneously certify a business they will jeopardize their reputation and may be open to law suit or other legal penalty. Remember this when you get frustrated with the requirements and attention to detail of a Certification process.

Here are the typical requirements of a Certification:

- The business is 51% or more owned by the proper classification (Minority, Woman, Veteran, Service Disabled Veteran or Disadvantaged Person).
- The Minority, Woman, Veteran or Disadvantaged Person owner(s) made an investment to obtain his/her ownership in the business seeking Certification.
- The business is managed on a day-to-day basis by the owner(s) that is of the proper classification (Minority, Woman, Veteran or Disadvantaged Person).
- The business is capable of providing the products and/or services it claims it can provide. This means your business has the proper license, equipment, people, training, building, vehicles or anything else that is necessary.
- If the Certification is for "disadvantaged" businesses you must prove that you meet that organization's/agency's description of disadvantaged. This includes one or more of the following:

1. Owner's individual personal worth is under a specific level (most use $750,000 as their level; the 8(a) SBA Program uses $250,000 as their level).
2. Owner is a member of a race or gender considered disadvantaged by that organization/agency.
3. Business is located in a geographic area that is considered disadvantaged or depressed.

Certification is one of the best tools in your tool box or briefcase or purse. Here are a few reasons why.

Certification has become a requirement instead of just a competitive advantage. As attention to the use of M/WBEs (Minority/Woman Business Enterprises) and DBEs (Disadvantaged Business Enterprises) increases so does the number of businesses claiming one or more of those designations. Many government agencies and businesses used to accept "self-declaration" as a qualifier for helping them meet their goals for the use of M/WBEs or DBEs. Now the number of businesses claiming those designations has become so large that the government agencies and corporations are more likely to require a Certification to verify, guarantee, validate that a business is truly a M/WBE , Veteran-Owned or DBE. Federal agencies still do not require Certifications; however, they normally expect their Prime Contractors to use Small Businesses, M/WBEs, Veteran Owned and DBEs as subcontractors and these Prime Contractors usually do require a Certification.

Certification demonstrates that you care. Having a Certification is proof that you qualify. It is also proof that you are willing to meet the requirements of a government agency, education institution or corporation. It is "part of the test" and shows that you are likely to be a good vendor. Another way to show you care is to obtain the Certification that your current or prospective Client/Customer prefers; even if you already have a different Certification. How do you know which Certification they prefer? Look at their website, determine which Certification their current vendors have or – ask your Prospect.

It is a badge you should wear (display) with pride. Including your Certification(s) on your website, business cards, brochures, digital information, etc. is a good way to demonstrate that you meet that requirement. Remember that your Certification is a qualifier, maybe a requirement, but it is not the only qualifier. Displaying it in the right places provides the information to those who need to know without seeming to say, "I expect your business because I am an M/WBE or DBE."

Being Certified may qualify you for exclusive opportunities. Sometimes government agencies, primarily federal or state, will do "set-asides" for a specific Small Business classification. In those cases you may be required to have a specific Certification to qualify.

Certification appeals to your Customers or Clients. Even if you provide products or services to individual consumers they may choose you because they know you are a Minority or Woman Owned Business. These people may not have a contract requirement or "spend" goal; however, they may prefer to use businesses that are owned by a Minority, Woman or Veteran. You can make the claim without the Certification, but that "Certified" stamp can elevate your status in their eyes.

One thing that hampers Small Businesses is not having the right, or best, Certification. There are a lot of Certifications. If you assume that a Certification does not apply to your business and do not do any research to find out you could suffer. It is important to determine which Certification or Certifications will help you. Following is some clarification about Certifications.

17

Most States offer some type of Certification for M/WBEs. Some States also require that the businesses they Certify are Disadvantaged (refer back to the descriptions of Disadvantaged under this Action). The State Certifications were developed primarily for state agencies and sometimes for local government agencies and schools. Some corporations will accept a State Certification, but most prefer a non-government Certification for meeting their own spend goals. However, if the corporation is a Prime Contractor for state agencies they may prefer the State's Certification.

Most State DOTs (Department of Transportation) have their own Certification. The Certification offered by State DOTs is for DBEs (Disadvantaged Business Enterprises). The requirements for this Certification are specifically set to meet federal guidelines because DOTs receive much of their funding from the federal government. This Certification was expanded in recent years to include all state and local government agencies and departments that receive federal transportation funding and it was named the UCP (Unified Certification Program).

Some local government entities offer their own Certification. Some cities, counties and even universities or school districts conduct their own Certifications.

Corporations often prefer private Certification. Most Corporations prefer Certifications from national private organizations because the requirements are the same for each business no matter where they are located. There are Certifications for Minority Owned Businesses and for Woman Owned Businesses. These organizations normally offer their Certified businesses training and access to Corporate buyers. It is important to know which Certification is preferred by your Corporate Clients, Customers and prospects.

Here are the primary organizations that offer a specific Certification:

- The US Veteran's Administration offers a "Verification" for Veteran-Owned and Service Disabled-Veteran Owned Businesses. The website for this government entity is: http://www.vetbiz.gov/vip/verify.htm.
- Minority-Owned Certification is offered by the local chapters of the private organization NMSDC (National Minority Supplier Development Council). The website is www.nmsdc.org.
- Woman-Owned Certification is offered by the following two private organizations:
  - o WBENC (Women's Business Enterprise National Council). The website is www.wbenc.org.
  - o NWBOC (National Women Business Owners Corporation) www.nwboc.org

When you look at your business and determine the things that will help you be successful Certification should at least be on the list for consideration. With it you can increase your opportunities; without it you may miss: an opportunity to qualify, a chance to compete on equal terms or an opportunity to be noticed. In tough economic times, every opportunity or advantage should be used.

Action #11

If any Certifications will be advantageous develop a schedule for applying.

Obtaining a Certification normally involves a great deal of paperwork and lot of time. Once you have determined if any Certifications are beneficial to you, then you will have to decide if the benefit is worth the time. Then, as with any complex, time-consuming undertaking you need to develop a schedule to insure that you get it done and that you do not miss anything.

The schedule does not have to be complicated. Use the "eat an elephant one bite at a time" method to tackle Certification application. Break the Certification application undertaking down into "bite-size" tasks, make a list of them and set a reasonable target date.

Following are some tips:

- When you prepare a Certification package, keep a copy of everything so that you can use it for re-certification or for a different Certification, because most organizations or agencies require similar documentation. If you know you need to obtain several Certifications do them all at once to save time and effort.
- Enlist someone to read your application material and to verify that you have gathered/prepared all the required documents on the "check list."
- Since many Certifications require copies of tax forms do the Certification application in conjunction with your annual tax preparation to save time.

Action #12

Establish a system to reward you and/or your staff when you accomplish important Actions.

The Actions in this book and those you have set for yourself and your business are designed to bring about positive results.

However, often times it helps you stay on track and persevere if you get rewards for incremental steps. Rewards do not have to be big, but they do have to have value to the recipient. Also, the more complicated or "unfun" the Action is, the more a reward will help.

As you incorporate the Actions of this book into your Marketing and Sales Plan, include rewards where feasible.

Here are a few illustrations:

- When an Action advises you to make contacts, plan to reward the person(s) who makes the contacts when a goal is reached.
- If an Action suggests completing online registrations, plan to provide a reward for every registration completed.
- When an Action requires research establish rewards for research as well as the activity that comes after the research is completed.
- Maybe even reward someone for preparation steps in order to move along to the actual Action.

Rewards can be tangible or they can by psychological. Following is a list of some typical and not-so-typical rewards that can be used.

- Movie Tickets
- Gift cards
- Breakfast/Lunch/treat
- Party
- Shirts, Hats
- Afternoon or day off
- Points toward gifts
- Golf or Spa certificates
- Certificate
- Recognition
- Award

Action #13

<u>Guard against spending too much time on "getting ready" instead of "doing".</u>

When doing something that is scary, risky, takes a lot of time, seems overwhelming or is boring/tedious it is tempting to put it off by "getting ready". Some common *delay tactics* that are easily disguised as *preparations* are:

- Buying supplies
- Making lists
- Getting others opinions
- Reading inspirational stories or articles
- Looking for an "easier" way
- "Finding" time

Whenever you are faced with something you know you should do to market your business and you find yourself struggling to get started or to make progress, ask yourself if you are postponing by pretending to prepare. To help yourself decide, plug your situation and your activities into one of the following examples:

Example A – Making a Dessert

You have to make a dessert for a pot-luck dinner. You really want to make something unusual and impressive. You look through your recipes, but you don't find one that quite fits. You ask some friends for suggestions. You look online for just the right dessert. You visit a bookstore or library and look through several books. You call a local bakery and ask for suggestions and prices. Now you have so much information you can't make a choice. Finally, the day before the event you pull out an old recipe you have used many times and rush to the store to get the ingredients. You prepare your tried-and-true dessert and take it to the pot-luck dinner. You are dismayed to find that three other people brought the same dessert. Your dessert certainly did not stand out, you wasted a lot of time and you have to take two-thirds of it home.

Example B – Building a Birdhouse

Your mother tells you she wants a birdhouse for Mother's Day. You think that building one for her will make it extra special. You search online for plans or kits, but there are so many choices. For inspiration you visit a local gift store that sells birdhouses. You go to a local hardware store and talk with a sales clerk about materials and kits. You buy some materials and a blueprint; you take them home to get started. You wait a few days until you can find time to build the birdhouse, but you can't seem to set aside enough time. Finally, the Saturday before Mother's Day you go to the gift store and buy one of their birdhouses. When your Mom opens the birdhouse, she smiles and says, "My friend Ella has one just like this."

Chapter 2
PHILOSOPHY

Action #14

<u>Understand the terms Supplier Diversity and Vendor Diversity and determine how they apply to your business.</u>

The terms Supplier Diversity and Vendor Diversity usually are accompanied by the words Policy or Program. This refers to a policy that, at the least, encourages the development and use of a diverse catalog of Suppliers/Vendors. The course of action may also be designed to drive the use of Diverse Vendors utilizing one or more of the following:

- Goals for the amount or percentage spent with Diverse Vendors
- Internal incentives and awards to staff for the use of Diverse Vendors
- Program(s) to seek out, assist, support and/or develop Diverse Vendors
- Definition of what the agency, business, or institution considers Diverse. Below is a list of business types that may be included in the definition of Diverse. Ownership must be 51% or more by the type of individual:
  - o Minority Owned
  - o Woman Owned
  - o Veteran Owned
  - o Service Disabled Veteran Owned

- o Small Business (additional information about this classification is provided on page 102).
- o Disadvantaged Business
- o Participation in organizations and events that provide opportunities to interact with Diverse Vendors
- Expectation that the major suppliers/vendors to the company or government/education entity also have a Supplier/Vendor Diversity policy and practice.

As a Diverse Vendor you have a built in marketing angle to use with a business, government agency or education institution that has a Supplier/Vendor Diversity Policy. This may not be the only or the best angle, but it is an option for you.

Action #15

Recognize that being a Small Business, Woman/Minority/Veteran Owned or a Disadvantaged Business is a *Marketing Angle* and not the foundation of your business or the basis of your marketing plan.

Your Small Business classification or Ownership status can open doors, give you a competitive advantage and help you gain access to opportunities or resources, but it will not get you business. Your best approach is usually "My business can provide you quality *(your product or service here)*. We can also help you meet your goals for the use of Small, Woman /Minority/Veteran Owned or Disadvantaged Business." If you lead with your Small or Ownership status instead of your product/service then it may appear that you expect to make the sale or get the contract solely based on that status or that you feel entitled to it. Although being a Small, Woman/Minority/Veteran Owned or Disadvantaged Business often increases your opportunities and your odds, it is not the most important factor to a Prospect. You still must meet their need.

It is important to understand all your possible marketing angles. List the assets and unique qualities of your business here so that you can begin looking for those other angles.

Here are some examples to help you get started:
- Delivery Services
- In-Home/In-Office Service
- Bonded
- 25 Years of Experience
- Multiple Locations
- Professional License or Certification
- Guarantee
- Recognized Expert (author, speaker, board/committee member, etc.)

Your top ten business assets and unique qualities:

1	
2	
3	
4	
5	
6	
7	
8	
9	
10	

Action #16

Know who your Customers/Clients are.

In doing research for organizations and centers that deal with small business development I always talk with local bankers about the obstacles for Small, Minority/Woman Owned and Disadvantaged Businesses. Almost every one of them tells me that the biggest obstacle for obtaining loans and to being successful is that the business owners do not know who their Customer/Client are (or will be). They further share that when most loan seekers are asked who their customers are, they start their answer with "all" or "any" and follow with a very general category. Here are some examples:

- ❖ All women
- ❖ Any teenager
- ❖ Any business owners
- ❖ All dog owners

According to the bankers it is very common for the response to this critical question to be "Anybody" or "Everybody." How simple marketing would be if this was true.

It is vital to know who your Customer/Client are so that you do not waste your time and money targeting people who are not your Customer/Client and so that you can convince lenders that you will be profitable.

In order to know if someone is actually a likely Customer/Client you must understand their buying criteria. This involves things like: needs, desires, willingness to pay, likelihood to act, obstacles to purchasing/using. It takes research to learn these things. But research beats wasted time, money and opportunities every time.

If you want to be sure you know who your Customer/Client are give yourself a test. Fill in the following form and share it with a lender, a small business counselor or a marketing professional. If you struggle to fill out the form or the person you share it with doesn't buy your explanation you need to do some research and clarification. A simple example entry is provided

PRODUCT or SERVICE AND CUSTOMER or CLIENT (Use a business type, not individual customer or client)	??	YOUR ANSWER	??	YOUR ANSWER
Example: Community Relations Services to the State Departments of Transportation	*What problem does your Customer/Client have that you can solve?*	*When work on roads and bridges causes detours and bad traffic situations DOTs need to inform and explain to the community and possibly hold community Q&A sessions*	*Why would they purchase this product/service from your business*	*DOTs need someone with local knowledge and contacts to ensure that information is shared in the most positive manner and that no one is left out.*

PRODUCT or SERVICE AND CUSTOMER or CLIENT (Use a business type, not individual customer or client)	??	YOUR ANSWER	??	YOUR ANSWER

Action #17

Understand that what you sell or provide is not what is important to your Prospect or Customer/Client.

What is important to Customers, Clients and Prospects is what you can do for them:

- What problem can you solve?
- What need can you meet?
- What difficulty can you help them avoid?
- What is their pain and how can you alleviate it?
- How can you help them increase revenue?
- How can you help them decrease expense, frustration or delay?
- How can you make their job/life easier?
- Can you reduce a cost, can you document that reduction?

List here the things you can do for your Prospects and Clients/Customers. Be sure you can identify it as a solution to a problem, answer to a need, avoidance of a difficulty, reduction of a cost, etc. If you cannot identify it in this manner you are probably not really addressing something that is important to them.

Your list:

What you can do for a Prospect, Customer or Client	Type (Solution, Answer, etc.)

What you can do for a Prospect, Customer or Client	Type (Solution, Answer, etc.)

Action #18

Recognize that relationships are the heart of buying and selling.

People still buy from people; Purchasers and Buyers are people. The best way to market and sell to people is to build a relationship with them. You and all your staff need to do business on a relationship basis. This will not only insure that you provide the highest level of customer service and increase the probability of repeat business, it is a pleasant and rewarding way of conducting business

A basic relationship can be built very quickly by concentrating on the needs and situation of the Prospect, Customer or Client. A relationship can be built over time by continuing the focus on the Prospect, Customer or Client and by doing things to show that your focus is. You really cannot expect to introduce yourself and your business to a Prospect and have them remember you a year later. You must make the effort to build the relationship by reminding them that you are out there waiting to meet their needs. You must find ways to show your willingness to meet their needs in the manner that they expect and maybe even require.

Being a Small, Woman/Minority/Veteran Owned or Disadvantaged Business is not who or what your business is, it is an aspect of your business. It may open the door or give you a competitive advantage, but you and your staff must develop a relationship and show how your status and your products/services provide benefits to your Prospect, Customer or Client.

Use the following forms to summarize your relationship with some Clients you were successful with and some Prospects that never turned into a Client/Customer.

Profitable Clients/Customers:

Profitable Client/Customer	Brief Description of Relationship

Prospect that never became a Client/Customer:

Prospect	Brief Description of Relationship

Use the information you learned from this exercise to guide you in the future development of relationships that will be profitable for you and the Client/Customer.

Action #19

Appreciate that the User of your product or service is your real target.

Many times in a purchasing or bidding situation you will be forced to deal with a Purchaser, Procurer or Buyer. That person (or department) is not the User of your product/services. They are in most cases the person enforcing the rules of purchasing/procurement. They are carrying out the wishes of the User to obtain a product or service and making sure that it is in keeping with the laws or internal guidelines. They may also be used to insulate the User from those "pushy" vendors. But the User is the one who establishes the criteria for the product or service. That means that your target for education, relationship, awareness, etc. is the User.

The User comes in many forms:
- Plant Manager
- School Principal
- Department Head
- Facilities Manager
- General Contractor
- Agency Director
- Etc., Etc.

Understanding of the Users world, needs, problems, obstacles, etc. will enable you to appropriately market to them. .

Users determine the specifics of a bid or RFP (Request for Proposal) or RFQ (Request for Quote or Request for Qualifications). They sometimes keep a "short list" of vendors/suppliers that they want to be sure gets an opportunity to respond to a bid, RFP or RFQ. The User normally makes the final purchasing decision or is involved in the evaluation process; they may even set the evaluation criteria.

Use the following form to examine a few past successful and unsuccessful sales/marketing situations and see if you can identify the actual User.

Profitable Clients/Customers:

Brief Description of Situation/Opportunity	User	Did you interact with the User?

Action #20

<u>Realize that you must identify and develop a relationship with the User of your products and services. Identify the User of your products and services at some of your target Prospects.</u>

Users decide if they need something, they determine if they have the funds to obtain it and they set the requirements for the bid, proposal and qualifications. They establish or influence the evaluation criteria. They sometimes decide on who gets to bid or propose, as long as they follow the laws or rules. If a Purchaser or Buyer is involved, that person or department adds the legal requirements and "does the shopping". If the User does not know your company and your product they may not know you have the solution to their problem or that your way of doing business fits best with their need. It is still necessary to get on the vendor/supplier list, but you must also get on the User's short list. Creating a relationship with the User will let you know if being Small, Woman/Minority/Veteran Owned or Disadvantaged is an effective marketing angle and, if not, what marketing angle is appropriate.

Look at a few current or expected opportunities and identify the User. Then try to find a way to get your information to the User or try to understand their needs so you can address it in your bid or proposal. Here is a form with an example to help you.

Brief Description of Situation/Opportunity	User
Trees are needed for a new city park.	*Parks & Recreation Dept.*

Action #21

<u>Accept the fact that the Purchasing/Procurement Staff are the rule keepers and they are not the User.</u>

In government agencies, at education institutions and school districts, and in businesses and corporations there has to be a department, office or person that insures that goods and services are obtained in an ethical and legal manner. That department, office or person is also responsible for seeing that the best interest of the agency, school or business is insured in each purchase or procurement and that the best price is obtained. This means that they establish and enforce "rules" or guidelines to accomplish these objectives. In the case of government and government supported education there are actually laws (local, state, federal) that must be followed in purchasing and procurement. An agency, school or business may also have policies to make sure Small and Disadvantaged businesses have an opportunity.

If you as a Small, Minority/Woman/Veteran Owned or Disadvantaged Business you should approach a Prospect or Customer/Client with respect for their rules and work within all their policies and cooperate in their programs for Small and Disadvantaged businesses. If you do you will increase your chances.

Take a close look at some past unsuccessful opportunities and determine if your lack of success was related in any way to you not understanding or not following the Purchasing/Procurement rules or guidelines. Use the following forms to write a brief description of the situation. This exercise will help you enforce this important factor so that you do not make the same mistake in the future; think of it like writing "I will not talk in class" on the blackboard a hundred times.

Situation #1

Situation #2

Situation #3

Action #22

Adopt the philosophy of always reading the "How to do business with" information on any Prospect.

More and more corporations, government agencies and education entities are providing information on their websites or in brochures or manuals about how to do business with them. This information often provides insight into what they buy or use. It will also tell you their process and, usually, their requirements (for qualifications, licenses, insurance, etc.). Being familiar with the "how to" information will help you

- Qualify the Prospect
- Identify benefits you can provide to the Prospect (remember that the benefits, not your products/services are what are important to the Prospect)
- Maximize your effort so you do not do unnecessary or detrimental things
- Determine if being Small, Minority/Woman/Veteran Owned or Disadvantaged is a major benefit, an added benefit or of no importance

Not being familiar with the "how to" information will cause you to make mistakes and can be interpreted as a non-responsive or even unqualified vendor. The business or government/education entity is the *customer* and they expect to be treated as such. Following their vendor guidelines shows respect and illustrates that you will be responsive to their needs on all levels.

There may also be legal reasons for their rules and processes. This is especially true of government agencies and education institutions. One good example of this "how to" information is the guide from the US Army at this website http://www.sellingtoarmy.info/User/Misc/13Steps.aspx.

Because many people like to "skip the directions" you will differentiate your business and increase your chances, by being familiar with and following the directions.

Action #23

Recognize that Subcontracting to government Prime Contractors could provide you excellent opportunities.

If you are in either of the following groups you should consider Subcontracting:

- My company is too small to compete successfully for government business.

- I would like to sell to the government, but I don't have time to deal with all the "red tape" – too many requirements, too complicated.
- I want to sell my products and services to large corporations.

Prime Contractors to government entities need Woman/Minority Owned Businesses and other Small and Disadvantaged businesses to meet contract and project requirements. When you act as a Subcontractor to the corporations that are Prime Contractors to government and education entities you help them satisfy their requirements and you benefit because:

- You do not have to prepare the whole bid or proposal
- You do not have to meet all the requirements of the request for bid or proposal
- You do not have to compete with larger businesses
- You can participate in large projects, thus increasing the number of opportunities
- You can develop a mutually beneficial partnership with a large corporation that could result in future opportunities

The current trend is for government entities to charge their Prime Contractors with involving Small, Woman/Minority/Veteran Owned and Disadvantaged Businesses in projects. This increases the need for Subcontractors.

Information on the SBA (Small Business Administration) goals is included in on page 53.

Make it a normal practice to automatically look for Subcontracting possibilities whenever you are searching for opportunities. Use Sub*Net* – see page 82.

Action #24

Understand your role if you are the Subcontractor.

If you are a Subcontractor, you actually have two masters – the Prime Contractor with whom you have an agreement and the end User. Even though the end User is the Customer/Client of the

Prime Contractor you are still responsible for providing some of the services or products. The Prime Contractor's obligations are also your obligations for the scope of your agreement with the Prime Contractor.

Following are a list of the most common problems Prime Contractors say they have with Subcontractors:

- Poor communication
- Miss deadlines on bids
- Do not have proper bonding or insurance
- Bite off more than they can chew (take on projects that they are not prepared to do)
- Miss deadlines on production, construction or delivery
- Fail to comply with safety requirements
- Go out of business in the middle of a job, usually because they are overextended financially
- Expect to get work because they are a Small, Minority/Woman/Veteran Owned or Disadvantaged Business
- Expect to get by with poor work because they are a Small, Minority/Woman/Veteran Owned or Disadvantaged Business
- Do not complete proper paperwork in a timely manner or, sometimes, at all

It is important to know what is expected of your business as the Subcontractor. It is equally important to incorporate the expectations into a written agreement so that confusion, finger pointing and problems are kept to a minimum. It is also vital that you share with all your employees and suppliers the expectations and time-frames of your Subcontracting Agreement.

Your role is to meet the expectations and do it in a way that pleases the End User and makes the Prime Contractor look good (and smart for hiring you). If you take this seriously you will improve your competitiveness and, therefore, your opportunities tremendously.

Action #25

<u>Look for ways to be the recipient of Outsourced functions and services.</u>

Take a close look at the way you market your products and services and consider "repackaging" them so that companies and government agencies see them as replacements for lost staff or more economical methods than in-house ones.

The generic term for using an outside company to provide a service or product that could be provided internally is "outsourcing." The term "outsourcing" is sometimes used to identify some other arrangements that many see as negative; an example is: using "cheap" off-shore labor and eliminating American jobs. However, outsourcing in this case is using Small Businesses for products and services instead of keeping them in-house. In times of economic distress that force layoffs, budget cuts and bankruptcy reorganizations outsourcing can help both the outsourcer and the outsource recipient.

The goals/requirements for the use of Small, Minority/Woman/Veteran Owned or Disadvantaged Businesses are not relaxed just because a project or function is outsourced. Actually outsourcing provides the larger corporations and government agencies an avenue to meet the goals and requirements for the use of these specific business types. Therefore it increases the possible opportunities for your business. In these situations the term "subcontracting" may be used instead of "outsourcing."

To help you understand how to incorporate this philosophy into your Marketing Plan here are some reasons that outsourcing may be desirable for companies and government agencies:

- Less expensive than an employee (especially with benefits)
- Reduced overhead (eliminate need for office space, warehousing, equipment, etc.)

- Avoidance of expensive over-time (using reduced regular staff to continue functions)
- Loss of revenue (unable to fill orders or fulfill contracts)
- Loss of grants or additional funding (cannot satisfy requirements)

Some of the characteristics the companies and government agencies (including schools) want to see in an outsource partner are:

- Flexibility to meet their time frames and requirements
- Willingness to accept small projects or orders
- Capability of matching their specifications and methods
- Willingness to provide temporary or sporadic services/products
- Ability to work on their site

Not all of these will be required in every situation.

To take advantage of outsourcing opportunities you must be looking for them. You should be watching news sources for announcements of layoffs and bankruptcies. You should be noticing trends of business or government types that are downsizing or struggling. When you find a business or government agency that is willing to outsource discover why and look for other prospects that share those reasons. Don't limit your prospecting to large companies or higher levels of government; other small businesses and local government agencies and schools may also need to outsource.

To help guide you in finding outsourcing opportunities here are some examples:

- Warehousing
- Accounting, Bookkeeping, Payroll or Tax Preparation
- HR (Human Resource) Services
- Sales Agents

- Temporary Staffing
- Storeroom Management
- Purchasing/Procurement
- Research, Data Gathering and Data Analysis
- IT Services
- Call Centers (Customer Service, Telemarketing, etc)
- Maintenance and Repair
- Facility/Property Management
- Janitorial Services
- Lawn Care
- Website Maintenance
- Order Fulfillment
- Printing/Copying
- Graphic Design, Desktop Publishing
- Marketing (PR, Media Contact)
- Inventory Control, Stocking
- Fund Raising
- Direct Mail Services (lead generation, reminders, fund raising, invitations, announcements, etc.)
- Specialized manufacturing or assembly
- Manufacturing services (metalworking, welding)
- Construction services
- Quality Assurance
- Safety Compliance
- Packing and shipping
- Translation Services
- Business Writing (reports, technical, etc.)
- Data Entry, Data Processing
- Forms Processing, Document Conversion
- Security
- Document Shredding (especially secure)
- Transcription (medical, legal, preservation)
- Training
- Telecommunications

Action #26

Acknowledge the fact that just because someone *should* do something does not mean he/she *will* do it.

Over the years of working in marketing and consulting to small businesses I have heard many versions of this conflict. Here are some examples:

- They *should* buy my product
- I *should* get a chance at that business
- He/She *should* use those services
- They *should* have considered that
- That *should* have been included in the requirements

It takes work, knowledge, perseverance and patience to convert *shoulds* into actions, especially the action you want. Make a list of some of the *shoulds* you have felt or said about your Prospects, Customers, Clients, Prime Contractors or anyone else negatively impacting your business opportunities and develop a strategy to convert those *shoulds* into a positive. Granted, this is not a critical exercise, but it could be fun and rewarding and it certainly will help keep you from getting caught up in what *should* be so you can concentrate on activity that will reap benefits.

SHOULD	CONVERSION STRATEGY

| | |
| | |

Action #27

<u>Treat marketing activities as you would treat a project for a Customer/Client.</u>

Your marketing activities are vital to your success. A good practice to insure marketing activities get the proper attention, time and effort is to treat them as you would a project for a Customer or Client. Following are some pointers:

- Plan
- Pay attention to detail
- Break the big picture down into appropriate steps/tasks
- Set a time line and be sure everyone involved is aware and in agreement
- Assign tasks to appropriate people
- Put tasks and key benchmarks on your calendar in keeping with the time line
- Hold yourself and others accountable
- Assess the success and determine needed improvements when the activity is completed

If you use a project management software or method for your Customer/Client projects, use it for your marketing activities. If you do not have a method, then develop one. A simple spread sheet and calendar may be sufficient as long as you have a method to develop, execute and track the elements of the activity.

Two benefits of treating marketing activities like projects:

1. Putting it in writing elevates its importance

2. Setting dates for steps/tasks and putting them on a calendar makes a commitment

Don't treat yourself and your business like the proverbial shoe cobbler treated his children.

Chapter 3
PREPARATION

Action #28

Be familiar with the SBA (Small Business Administration) Goals for use of small and diverse businesses by the federal government and its prime contractors.

The SBA works with federal agencies, local government agencies that receive federal funds and prime contractors on projects/contracts that involve federal funding. They help set the goals for the percentage of the project/contract that will be spent with Diverse Vendors and monitor compliance with the goals. You can see details on the SBA website at: http://www.sba.gov/aboutsba/sbaprograms/goals/SBGR_2006_GOA LING_OVERVIEW.html but here is a summary of the minimum goals by type of diverse business:

- Small Business - 23%
- Woman-Owned Small Businesses (WBE) - 5%
- Small Disadvantaged Businesses (SDB) – 5%
- Service Disabled Veteran Owned Small Businesses (SDVOSB) – 3%
- HUBZone Small Businesses – 3% (the specific requirements to be a HUBZone Small Business are explained on the SBA Website).

If you fall into one of these categories you need to consider that you might be able to sell your products and services to federal agencies or local government agencies that receive federal funds. Because Prime Contractors (the company that actually signs the contract) are held to these same goals you may be able to serve as a Subcontractor, supplying part of the products or services on a large government project or contract. A Prime Contractor must show how they will meet these goals in their proposal and then follow through by actually meeting those goals. The goals were established to encourage, almost require, the use of diverse businesses.

This knowledge is beneficial in developing a marketing plan by helping you identify Prospects and understand if your ownership status is a viable marketing angle.

Action #29

Be familiar with the Supplier Diversity goals of the state and local governments, state supported schools, school districts and corporations that are in the geographic area you can serve.

State and local governments, state supported schools and local school districts typically use a goal of 10% as a rule of thumb. The goal may be higher or lower, depending on the specific project and the perceived availability of Small, W/MBE or Disadvantaged Businesses.

The goals of corporations vary according to their business type and Customers/Clients. If they provide products/services to a government or education entity or to another corporation that has Supplier Diversity goals, then their goal percentage will probably mirror that of their Customer/Client. If they use products/services that are not typically supplied by Small, Minority/Woman/Veteran Owned or Disadvantaged Businesses then their goals may be low.

If you know the goals then you can appropriately incorporate them into your Marketing Plan and efforts. The goals also give you an indication of how to use the marketing angle of Small, Ownership or Disadvantaged status. The higher the goal and the more prominently it is published the more important it is to them.

The goals are normally published in the Supplier/Vendor Diversity Policy. The Policy is usually available on their websites if they are serious about meeting the goals.

Action #30

<u>Determine the geographic area in which you can profitably provide your products or services.</u>

Two old sayings can help you with this determination, they are:

- Don't make promises you can't keep
- Don't bite off more than you can chew

Your profitable geographic area may be your city, your county, a 5 county area, your state, 3 states, the US, etc. How you determine your profitable geographic area is very dependent on your type of business. It is important to make this determination so that you do not spend time, money and effort searching for opportunities in the wrong places. You will likely need to do this again in the future as your situation changes and conditions vary (i.e. gas prices). If you did this in your Business Plan take a look at it to be sure it is finite enough to guide your research and marketing efforts.

Here is a simple equation to aid you, highlighted items are geographically specific:

Determine the price you can charge (may be influenced by the geographic area because a government client sometimes sets a maximum price or requires preferential discounts; competition or other local factors may also influence price)

Subtract the following:

- Cost of providing or producing product (i.e. hourly rate, cost of material + labor, etc.)

- Cost of delivery (shipping, travel to provide service, etc.)

- Prorated overhead

- *Taxes if applicable (include local taxes, local business license [sometimes required to do business in a specific city/county], etc.)*

- *Cost of getting or selling (cost of producing proposal, time involved, travel time and cost, etc)*

- *Other costs associated with providing product/service in the specific geographic area*

Profit *(If this is a positive figure decide if it is positive enough; if it is negative – you do the math).*

Action #31

Develop a one-pager on your company.

Because Prospects and Customers are interested in what you can do for them, not what you do or sell, you need to have an appropriate document that will tell them. They may be impressed by your brochures, but they will be persuaded by your one-pager. Here are some reasons they like one-pagers:

- It's easier to keep in a file or notebook
- It provides facts instead of art
- It can be emailed – to them and by them
- It is short and to-the-point
- It can be used for future reference when they are looking for vendors

You may have multiple one-pagers that have the same basic information, but also include specifics for the customer or type of customer. Here are some things that can be included:

- Short paragraph about the products and services you offer stated in a way that shows how it applies to the intended reader
- List of some recent projects and the need/problem they addressed (with contact names if you have permission)
- Certifications, Licenses (including Woman/Minority/Veteran Owned or Disadvantaged)

- Your contact information
- Your logo, your colors, but nothing flashy

Think of the one-pager as your company's resume.

If you can't get it on one page, print it front and back, but try hard to do it on one page. It may be psychological, but Prospects and Customer/Clients are more likely to take time to read something that is one page than even look closely at something that is longer. You may want to attempt to do the one-pager as the inside of a brochure. Also be sure that you have an electronic version because many people would rather have it in that form so that they can keep it in a database and pass it on to others.

Consider developing a basic one-pager that you can modify to suit specific Prospects. For instance, if you want to sell your products/services to schools then you may want to have two versions – one for K-12 schools and one for colleges/universities.

Note: Be sure to have some people outside the company read it to check for understanding and errors.

On the following pages is a guide to help you develop a one-pager.

Your Company Name

Company Address

Company Phone Number

Web Site

Primary Contact Name: *Your Company Primary Contact*

Primary Contact Phone Number: *Your Primary Contact Number*

Primary Contact Email Address: *Your Primary Contact Email*

Primary Contact Fax Number: *Your Primary Contact Fax*

Located in _____ County

Products or Services Provided:

List only the products and/or services you provide that would be of interest to this specific Prospect or department. Be clear and concise. Present them in a way that demonstrates how they apply to the recipient of this document. Do this with product/service name, description or example. Use their language or identifiers as often as possible. This is the primary place you will customize to suit the audience.

Federal Tax ID #: *List the Federal Tax ID (FEIN) here. If you use your Social Security Number instead, then use the term Social Security # instead of Federal Tax ID # and provide it here. Remember that it is a security risk to provide your Social Security #, FEIN is better.*

NIGP, SIC and/or NAICS codes: *List codes that apply to your products/services here. Explanation on NIGP is provided on page 12, SIC and NAICS on page 11.*

Professional Licenses or Certifications: *If a professional license (i.e. contractor, speech therapist) or certification is required or advantageous then list it here. Include special certifications or designations such as LEED or ISO.*

Certifications: *List Certifications your company has, include certification name (i.e. WBE [Woman Business Enterprise] or DBE [Disadvantaged Business Enterprise], etc.), Certifying Agency/Organization, Certification Number.*

Business License #: *If your business is located in a city you are likely required to have a business license, provide the City name, business license number and expiration date. Some Counties also require a Business or Operations License. Include the city/county name. Note: Some cities will require that you obtain some type of license (business, vendor, temporary) in order to do business with you. Be sure that you are familiar with and meet the requirement or state that you will meet it if awarded any bid/contract.*

Invoice Payment Terms: *State your payment terms, i.e. Net 30, 10the of month, due upon receipt, etc*

References: *One or two applicable references can be provided here, but this will only be beneficial if they are recognizable and relative to the entity you are sending this to. This is another place that you can customize for the recipient.*

Try to keep this information to one page. Brochures are usually not desired. If something cannot be explained in this one page form, you can provide an additional page with details and reference it under Products or Services; however the additional details are of more interest to the people/department that will actually use your products/services. Remember that this information page is directed to the purchasing office which primarily wants to classify and preliminarily qualify your business.

If you do business in your own name then use the template on the following page and refer back to the previous letter template for explanations on the items to include.

Your Name
Your Address
Your Phone Number

Email Address: *Your Email*

Fax Number: *Your Fax*

Located in _____ County

Products or Services Provided:

List only the products and/or services you provide that would be of interest to this specific Prospect. Be clear and concise.

Social Security #:

NIGP, SIC and or NAICS codes:

Professional Licenses or Certifications:

Certifications:

Business License #:

Invoice Payment Terms:

References:

Use this form to develop your own one-pager.

_____

_____

_____

Primary Contact Name:

_____

Primary Contact Phone Number:

_____

Primary Contact Email Address:

_____

Primary Contact Fax Number:

_____

Located in _____ County

Products or Services Provided:

_____

_____

_____

_____

Federal Tax ID #: _____.

NIGP Codes: _____

SIC Codes: _____

NAICS Codes: _____

Professional Licenses or Certifications: _____

_____

Certifications: _____

_____

Business License:

_____

Invoice Payment Terms: _____

References:

    1. _____

_____

    2. _____

_____

    3._____

_____

Actions 32 & 33

Note: These two Actions are listed together because they are so closely coupled.

<u>Use an email address that has your business name after the @.</u>

<u>Get a website</u>

It is much more professional and makes a better impression if your email includes your business name as the URL or host. For example <u>jamievendor@yourbusinessname.com</u> is much better than <u>yourbusinessname@internethost.com</u> (examples of Internet Hosts are Hotmail, Google, AOL, Yahoo, AT&T, etc.). This means that you will need to have a website, which is vital if you plan to attempt to do business with large businesses, government agencies and education institutions. This does not really have anything to do with your Small Business or Ownership status; however, it is a common blunder. Unfortunately potential Prospects view the lack of a website as a hesitation to commit to a "being in business." Having your business name in your email address is an automatic indication that you have a website. If you do not have a website get one, you unequivocally need one.

There are hosting companies that offer websites for as little as $10 a month. Most websites come with at least one email address that includes the website name, thus enabling you to have an email address with your company name after the @. The number of pages or amount of data space (remember pictures and videos take up much more data space than words) directly affects the cost. Many hosting companies also offer for additional fees such services as:

- Website templates (so you can fill in blanks and have a professional look)
- Additional email addresses
- Shopping Cart services including payment (PayPal, credit card) so you can do on-line selling

- Search maximization and/or advertising
- Technical Assistance
- Design Assistance
- "Hit" counts (Hit = number of times someone visits your website or a specific page on the site)
- Webinar or other online conferencing capability

You can always start out small with a website and add capabilities or space as you have need and can afford.

Caution: Because websites are a mystery to those not familiar with the technology; there are people/companies who will make promises for services that they cannot truly provide or guarantees for getting traffic to your site that are challenging, if not impossible, to meet. Be sure you ask for and check references before committing.

Action #34

Include your Minority/Woman/Veteran Owned or Disadvantaged Certifications or Small Business status on your website.

Don't skip this action if you do not have a website. *If you do not have a website you need to establish one immediately. There are companies that will host your website and provide you templates that allow you to do-it-yourself for as little as $10 a month. Do a web search using the key words "hosted website with templates". Additional information is provided in this book on page 63.*

Where and how you will list your Certifications or Small Business status depends on the design of your website. Do remember that if you have them listed on a page other than the first/home page, you should have a link on the first page to the place they are listed and the link should be identified as Woman, Minority, Veteran Owned or Disadvantaged Certifications. If you are certified by an organization that allows you to use their logo, then by all means do so. If the agency/organization provides a

Certification number, include it with the certification name and agency/organization.

Action #35

Incorporate your Small, Disadvantaged or Minority/Woman/Veteran Owned status and marketing angle into your Marketing Plan.

Remember that your Small or Ownership status is **not** your Marketing Plan. It is a marketing angle and tool, so it should be appropriately incorporated into a comprehensive Marketing Plan. Incorporating it into your Marketing Plan will insure that you maximize and capitalize on the Small, Disadvantaged or Ownership status. This status can provide a competitive advantage, open doors, gain attention and make you eligible for specific opportunities if you use it appropriately and at every opportunity. Look at your Marketing Plan and find ways to use your Small, Disadvantaged or Ownership status to enhance your efforts and expand your opportunities, but do not base your plan on your status. If you are truly *working* your plan you will be adapting and adjusting it frequently, be sure you fit in your status suitably.

Here are some examples of how to incorporate:

- If your Marketing Plan includes seeking Subcontracting opportunities on projects too large for your company to handle alone then adjust your plan so that you are identifying Prospects that need Subcontractors with your Small or Ownership status to meet their contract requirements. (i.e. Highway General Contractor that needs a Minority Owned Subcontractor who does curbing.)
- If you are an architectural or construction firm but cannot tackle large building construction projects and do not have the resources to work outside your local area, you can include in your Marketing Plan efforts to promote your firm

as a local representative for large General Contractors with no presence in the geographic area you can cover.

- As you look for a way in to the purchasing process for a large corporation consider entering through the Supplier Diversity "door "if they have a diversity policy. As you do your research on a particular corporation, determine if they have a Supplier Diversity contact (sometimes called Small Business Liaison). Then use that contact and any registration process to gain introduction to the company and its purchasers.

Take one component of your Marketing Plan and think through a way your Small or Ownership status can help or enhance that component.

Marketing Plan component: _____

_____

Way to utilize Small or Ownership status in this component:

_____

_____

_____

Action #36

Prepare a template letter requesting to be placed on "Vendor" or "Bidder" list.

Formulate this for cities, counties, school districts and other government and education entities that do not have a Vendor Registration form (online or paper). Following is a basic letter. Include as a second sheet your one-pager. (The one-pager is covered on page 56 of this book). You can modify the letter and one-pager to suit your Prospect.

Use your stationery with the address and phone number on it, but still include the information as shown in the following example so that it is easy to see.

1st Page

Ms. June Purchaser

City of Opportunity

24 Main Street

Opportunity, XX

Dear Ms. Purchaser,

 I am writing to request that my company, *Your Company Name*, be placed on your vendor/bidder list.

 I/We provide XXX and YYY. We/I are certified by ZZZ as a Woman (*or Minority or Veteran*) Owned Business. (*or "We meet the SBA qualifications as a Small Business.)*

 Detailed information is provided on the attachment. Please let me know if you need additional information.

 Thank you for your consideration,

Your Name, Title

- -

2nd page

Include your one-pager (see page 56.)

If your business name is your name use this letter template and replace the words "my company" with the word "I".

Once you have already completed your one-pager as detailed on page 56 then prepare your basic letter on the following form. Again be sure to replace "my company" with "I" if your business name is your name. Remember to customize the letter and one-pager before you send it to a specific Prospect. If your Prospect prefers email it is easy to adapt the letter to email text once you have the letter developed.

If you operate as a company:

Date _____

M_____

_____

_____

_____, ____

Dear M_____,

I am writing to request that my company, _____, be place on your vendor/bidder list.

I/We provide _____ and _____. We/I are certified by _____ as a _____ Business.

Detailed information is provided on the attachment. Please let me know if you need additional information.

Thank you for your consideration,

_____, _____

Action #37

Develop and use a Customer/Client Contract that includes a Scope of Work.

A contract serves many purposes. Here are some of the common ones:

- Protect your business
- Establish expectations
- Avoid misunderstandings
- Assign responsibilities
- Clarify consequences
- Provide for recourse

A contract may be a multi-page document drawn up by an attorney, a fill in the blank form from a legal services website or a statement on a store receipt. The form and language depends on the specifics of your business. But no matter what the form, it is important to "put it in writing."

A Scope of Work is normally used for services and outlines what your business will do/provide, when, sometimes how and the cost. This document helps your Client/Customer understand what to expect from you and avoids them assuming or attempting to add tasks that were not in the original negotiation. Sometimes it is advisable to include in the Scope of Work the expectations or responsibilities of the Customer/Client. This can be important because your tasks may be dependent on them completing or providing something. Here is an illustration: You are conducting research and have committed to interview a group of people. You cannot interview those people until your Client provides you a list of names and contact information. Your Scope of Work should show that your task is dependent on the Client completing their task.

Following is an example of a very simple Scope of Work.

Scope of Work for
Tasteful Jewelry Company
Customer Satisfaction Study

Consultant will provide the following services:

- Hold up to 3 onsite meetings with Client to learn about the products, services and policies of the company.
- Interview 25 customers in the store
- Conduct in-store surveys on four occasions for 5 hours each (specific dates to be determined in meeting with Client)
- Survey attendees at March meeting of two women's organizations.
- Compile results of interviews and surveys
- Prepare Customer Satisfaction Study Report by May 30

All dates are dependent on the Client providing stipulated information in a timely manner.

Client will:

- Explain product line, services and policies to Consultant before any interviews or surveys can be conducted
- Provide Consultant adequate space in the store for interviews and surveys
- Provide list of meetings of women's groups that can be contacted by Consultant to participate in the survey
- Provide giveaway with store logo for Consultant to provide to survey participants

Cost:

The total cost for this project is $100,000. This cost includes all expenses except the giveaways that are to be provided by Client.

Payment will be made in the following manner:

- $20,000 due upon execution of contract
- $40,000 at half-way point of project (*it is preferable to state a*

---

specific date)
- $40,000 upon delivery of Customer Satisfaction Study Report

Consultant will provide invoices at appropriate intervals.

Consultant Signature _____

Client Signature _____

Date _____

A Scope of Work can also be incorporated into a proposal because it clearly lays out what you will do, when and what the cost is. This is likely to either move negotiations along more quickly or prod the Prospect to demonstrate if they are serious or not.

Even though a "Scope of Work" is used primarily in the provision of services, it can also be used if installation or implementation is included in the sell of equipment, software, etc.

If your business is retail or direct to consumer you may want to include your "Scope of Work" on your receipt. This would be something that applies directly to your business and sets conditions and/or expectations. Here are a few examples:

- Only exchanges for store credit are provided if item(s) is returned.
- One year warranty is provided with conditional limitations.
- No returns accepted after 60 days from purchase.

Use the form on the following page to develop a Scope of Work for a project you plan or hope to do. Then use that as a template for future projects.

Scope of Work for

Client Name _____

Project Name _____

Consultant will provide the following services:

- _____
- _____
- _____
- _____

All dates are dependent on the Client providing stipulated information in a timely manner.

Client will:

- _____
- _____
- _____
- _____

Cost;

The total cost for this project is $_____. This cost includes all expenses except _____

Payment will be made in the following manner:

- $_____ due upon execution of contract
- $_____ on _____
- $_____ upon completion of _____

Consultant will provide invoices at appropriate intervals.

Consultant Signature _____

Client Signature _____

Date _____

Action #38

Create and utilize a Non-Disclosure Agreement

It is very important to use a Non-Disclosure Agreement as a part of your contract with a Customer/Client, a partner or a Prime Contractor. The purpose of this agreement is to be sure that your information, processes, knowledge, etc. cannot be used or shared without your permission. For most businesses a Mutual Non-Disclosure is the best form since it not only protects your business, but it also shows that you will protect the information, processes, customers/clients, etc of the other party.

Use of this type of agreement will provide you the following benefits:

- Protect your business
- Illustrate that you are a "serious" business person
- Show you respect the privacy and confidentiality of your Customer/Client, partners or Prime Contractor
- Avoid misunderstandings
- Provide legal recourse

This agreement needs to be legally binding. At the least you want to adopt one from a website or book/CD that provides other legal contracts. To be sure your agreement is binding and suits your specific needs you may want to have one drawn up by an attorney.

Once you have this agreement, do not hesitate to use it. If you explain that you always use it and that it protects the other party as well, people will accept it; sometimes they are even impressed.

Action #39

Create and use a contract with partners and Prime Contractors

Having a contract that clearly defines the roles and responsibilities, time frames and financial arrangements makes any partnership work more smoothly. The contract can help avoid delays, misunderstandings and missed deadlines. It protects and benefits all parties.

Some Prime Contractors have a standard contract they use with Subcontractors. If this is the case you will have to accept the Prime's contract.

You may want to develop and use a standard contract or you may find it advantageous to draw one up for each individual partnership. You will have to determine what suits your specific situation.

Do not assume that because you know someone or are related to someone that you do not need a contract. Business partnerships gone wrong can ruin friendships and strain family relations.

Here is a personal story that illustrates the need for a contract in writing.

> I had known and worked with an engineering firm for several years. I introduced one of the Principals to an opportunity with a city government. Because I had information, contact and expertise I was to work on the project as a subcontractor. We verbally agreed on a price and started the project. After a few weeks we met and determined that it was going to take more of my time to do the necessary research. I said I could do the research, but would need a larger portion of the revenue. The Principal (and friend) said that was no problem and agreed to pay me the additional amount. When the project was complete the Principal informed me that he would only be able to pay me the original agreed on amount. To add insult to injury when I met with someone in a neighboring city government they showed me a report that my "friends" engineering firm had prepared for them at a price about three

times that of the project I had subcontracted on about a year earlier. The report included a lot of the material I had researched and prepared for the original project. They had turned my material into a boiler plate report and I was not receiving any royalties. I found out a few months later that the engineering firm had made a proposal to yet another city government to do the same study; likely they would have used my material again.

The moral is: Put it in writing and get signatures.

Action #40

Determine if your likely Prospects require Bonding and/or Insurance and make arrangements to comply.

Bonding and insurance are something many government, education and corporate Prospects require of any vendors. These requirements are for risk mitigation – minimizing the risk of your Prospect, Client or Customers in doing business with a vendor. The risk could be a law suit, a fine, loss of a contract or other negative impact.

Now take a deep breath before you start crying foul because a Prospect, Client or Customer expects you to minimize their risk by paying for a Bond or Insurance. Remember that they do not want to be held accountable for your mistakes, accidents, lack of knowledge or ability, failure to do the work or comply with a law or anything else that causes a risk. Unfortunately if one party takes all the risk they have no leverage to insure that a vendor, service provider or subcontractor holds up their end of the agreement or, worse, they could end up financially unable to operate because of the risks listed in the previous paragraph.

Exactly what bonding or insurance a government, education or business entity requires varies according to their specific needs and perceived risks. Normally they are very specific about what they require.

Some places to find the requirements:

- Government/Education RFB (Request for Bid) or RFP (Request for Proposal) – it pays to take a look at a RFB or RFP to see the requirements
- Website of government, education or business entity
- Ask the Purchasing, Procurement or Supplier Diversity department or contact
- "Guide to Doing Business" handbook/document

Bonding and Insurance can be an expensive pill to swallow, but there are some options and resources:

- The SBA (Small Business Administration) has a program to help small and emerging contractors with Surety Bonds. Details can be found at this link: http://web.sba.gov/faqs/faqindex.cfm?areaID=20
- Some Prime Contractors are willing to absorb the Bond/Insurance requirement or expense for their subcontractors because they need Small, Minority/Woman/ Veteran Owned or Disadvantaged Businesses to meet their Supplier Diversity goals or requirements.
- Some government agencies have funds or resources to assist small businesses in meeting Bonding requirements. For example many State DOTs (Departments of Transportation) via Federal funding are able to assist their certified DBEs (Disadvantaged Business Enterprises) with this requirement.
- Some Centers for Small, Minority/Woman/Veteran Owned or Disadvantaged Businesses have funds or resources to assist their participants with Bonding and Insurance requirements.
- In some instances, because of the specifics or size of the purchase, job, project, etc., the government, education or business entity may relax or eliminate the Bonding or Insurance requirements.

Just be careful that you do not ignore this important factor as you are doing research, networking, prospecting and proposing. It would be very frustrating to spend a lot of time identifying and cultivating an opportunity and then find out you could not take advantage of it because you did not take into account Bonding and Insurance. This is no time to practice those tempting concepts of "maybe if I ignore it, it will go away" or "gee, I didn't know."

Chapter 4
PROSPECTING

Action #41

<u>Choose a State Agency in your home state that is likely to have need of your products and services and determine which departments, programs or offices within that Agency are good Prospects.</u>

You cannot research all the state agencies or departments of your state government at once. Therefore, you need to choose the most likely agency (or department or office) and begin to research the operations and needs within to determine where your actual Prospects are. This method is a good way to familiarize yourself with the procurement laws and processes and the supplier/vendor diversity policy and philosophy of your state. This is two-for-one method that utilizes the identification and qualification of a potentially real Prospect to also learn state procurement as a whole. Keep in mind that although agencies and departments are supposed to adhere to the state goal for the use of M/WBEs (Minority/Woman Business Enterprises) or Small Businesses, they are normally allowed to use their own method of reaching that goal and are rarely rewarded if they meet the goal or penalized if they do not meet it.

Sometimes you will know that a State Agency or Institution needs/uses your particular products or services, but you still need to understand the specifics and conditions associated with that need to know if the agency/institution qualifies as a real Prospect. Other times you will need to better understand the functions of the agency/institution in order to know what they need. It does take research to identify and qualify Prospects, but it also takes time to indiscriminately send out information and make contacts in the hopes of running across some Prospects.

Do not assume that you have to be located in the state's capitol city to do business with a state agency or department. Most have locations or people throughout the state. Determining where the product or service must be provided should be part of the qualification process. It is important to understand the geographic area you can serve because this will play a significant role in deciding what State Agency is a good Prospect for you. More information on determining if you can profitably serve a specific geographic area is provided on page 55 of this book.

Following are some examples to help guide your research. Keep in mind that you will not know the situation/need/condition if you do not do research on that department.

Agency/Institution	Situation/Need/Condition	Prospect?
Health Department	Need Site Inspectors in each of its 10 Regions. You can provide the service in 3 of the Regions.	If the Health Department will consider providers that can serve one or some of their Regions instead of all 10, then it may be a good Prospect. If they want one provider, you may be able to serve as a Subcontractor to a Prime Contractor that can serve all 10

Agency/Institution	Situation/Need/Condition	Prospect?
		Regions so actually gets the contract. You also may be able to partner with other Small Businesses on a joint or collaborative proposal; however, one of the companies will likely have to serve as the Prime Contractor
State University	Is not located in your geographic area but needs a product that you can provide.	If you can provide the product and still make a reasonable profit taking into consideration the things outlined on page 55, then this may be a good Prospect. This is not a good Prospect if you are considering losing money in order to build reputation; other state schools and agencies will expect the same price, so there is

Agency/Institution	Situation/Need/Condition	Prospect?
		no way to make up your loss.
Department of Mental Health	The department holds annual events in each of its offices to recognize community leaders. The budget is limited and the department wants consistency.	The limited budget and need for consistency make it more likely that one vendor will be chosen. If you can conduct the events in all the geographic areas and work within a limited budget, then this may be a good Prospect.

Note: It is very important to register in the state vendor database before making contact with any agency, department, office or institution. More details about this registration are provided on page 127.

Action #42

Establish a practice for checking the Sub-*Net* website for Subcontracting opportunities.

The SBA (Small Business Administration) hosts a website where Federal Government Prime Contractors can post their needs for Subcontractors. The website address is http://web.sba.gov/subnet. This website does allow you to search by NAICS, keywords (description) and state. If you want to take advantage of this resource you must check it often because there is not a schedule for posting opportunities; Prime Contractors post the need when they have it and the interval for response may be short.

You should put a note on your calendar (paper or electronic) to check the site about every 2 weeks. If you check it that often it will only take a few minutes each time. This is certainly a task that can be delegated as long as the person checking the website knows what he/she is looking for.

Action #43

Once you have identified government and education Prospects develop a process to watch for grants they receive that could require them to utilize W/MBEs.

Sometimes grants or funding that comes from Federal Agencies or foundations includes stipulations that a specific percentage of the project/program expenditures be spent with Small or Disadvantaged Businesses or M/WBEs. Usually notices of these grants are posted on the recipient's websites and they may be reported in local media. Where there is a need; there is an opportunity.

Here are a few suggestions:
- Schedule regular online visits to their website and look under:
  o News or Press Releases
  o Announcements
  o School (as in school of engineering or nursing), department, agency, initiative, center, etc. that you have targeted
  o Web page for the Grants Department, Coordinator, Director, etc.
- Watch local newspapers and television news
- Watch the websites of local newspapers, television news, news sites, bloggers, etc that may announce grants

Remember that the recipient will be proud of receiving the grant so they are likely to contact the media and announce it any place they can.

This is another item that should be put on your calendar so that you actually do it on regular basis, not when you get around to it or it may be too late.

Action #44

Use government and education entities Existing Contracts or "Term Contracts" to find Subcontracting opportunities.

An existing contract is simply what the word suggests – a contract that already has been executed, is in existence. A "Term Contract" is a purchase contract for products or services that continues for a specified fixed period of time; in the case of government a typical Term Contract is for one to five years, sometimes the contract terms will be for one year with automatic extensions of 2 to 4 years if conditions do not change and/or specifications continue to be met.

The businesses that have been successful in securing government and education contracts likely have two desires – retain/renew the contract and obtain new contracts. Very often they need Subcontractors to do either. Remember that the responsibility of meeting the goals for the use of Small, Minority/Woman/Veteran Owned and Disadvantaged Businesses is often passed down to the Prime Contractor – the business that has the contract. Even if they have Subcontractors on their existing contracts, that could change. Also, they could need new Subcontractors on future opportunities. You need make your business known to the Prime Contractors.

Most state government agencies and public universities provide online access to their Term and Existing Contracts. Some local governments and school districts do, too. If online access is not provided, you can probably find out from the Purchasing or

Procurement staff at the government entity or school district. But be sure to explain that you would like to approach the existing contractor about Subcontracting possibilities so that the Purchaser understands what you are doing. They will normally be helpful because it is in their best interest for their contractors to use appropriate Subcontractors.

There are two ways to find Existing and Term Contracts on a website:

1) Watch for bids and follow them until the contract is awarded. Government entities and government supported schools must post their contract awards. The information on the business receiving the contract award will not be in great detail, but does normally provide a contact person, address and phone number.

2) Look at the state government's purchasing/procurement web pages to find their Term or Existing Contracts. They must post this information with adequate details to identify the contractor and terms. Some specific State Agencies or state supported schools may maintain online information about their own contracts. Larger cities, counties and school districts may also post this information online.

Once you have identified Prospects then look at their Existing and Term Contracts and follow through to make contact with the appropriate contract holders about Subcontracting opportunities.

Action #45

Search for opportunity trends in the "Want Ads."

When you are looking for new markets or fresh ways to repackage your services look at the job postings in the newspaper and online job search sites. Also attend job fairs. The indicators and trends shown in job postings can help guide you to possible outsourcing opportunities. If businesses, and even government and education, are having a hard time finding certain professionals they may be willing to contract with your business for those services. Here are some examples:

- School Districts are having trouble finding Speech Therapists so they will consider contracting with a company that can provide the Therapists.
- Businesses advertising for clerical and administrative staff may consider using a temporary staffing company or a company that provides Virtual Assistants. In tough economic times this is even more likely because of the cost of office space.
- Companies seeking drivers may be good Prospects for trucking, hauling or delivery companies.

The fact that you are a Small, Woman/ Minority/Veteran Owned or Disadvantaged Business may be an extra incentive for them to use your services instead of hiring someone, because you can help fulfill a goal or contract requirement for using Small, W/MBEs and Disadvantaged businesses.

If you know of a job opening, don't hesitate to contact the business or government/education entity or send them a proposal, especially in economically difficult times. Or you can contact similar agencies, schools or businesses in case they have the same needs. Be sure to do your homework first so you will understand what the company, agency or school does and how you could fit in. Also, get an idea of what it would cost for an employee (salary, benefits, training, etc) compared to outsourcing the service to your company. You can use those same job posting sites to get an idea of salary; other sources for salary and benefit cost are the US Bureau of Labor and Statistics and your state departments of employment and/or commerce.

Once again this task needs to be assigned to someone and put on their calendar. Maybe it's a regular Monday morning or Friday afternoon duty.

Action #46

Use organizations that focus on Supplier Diversity to identify Prospects.

There are several organizations that provide support, certification, events and/or resources to facilitate Supplier Diversity. They usually have membership of Woman Owned, Minority Owned or other Disadvantaged businesses. They also have corporate members. Corporations that join and participate in organizations focused on Supplier Diversity are potential Prospects for you. The fact that they are willing to pay the membership fee (corporate membership is much higher than that for a W/MBE) demonstrates that the matter is important to them. Their degree of participation in the organization is also an indicator of how serious they are about utilizing Small Businesses, W/MBEs and other Disadvantaged businesses. Many corporations that participate in these organizations also include Small Businesses in their Supplier Diversity execution. When determining their degree of participation look to see if a corporation's representative:

- Serves on the Board or a Committee
- Attends meetings regularly
- Participates in Matchmaking or Networking events
- Has been a long time Member
- Sponsors events

Note: Unfortunately there are businesses, government agencies and education institutions that will assert simple membership in these organizations as complete fulfillment of Supplier Diversity; they feel that if they join the organization they have done their part. Therefore, it is important to only utilize simple membership as an identifier, not an automatic qualifier. Their level and type of participation can assist you in qualifying them as a true potential Prospect for your business.

Following are some of the Supplier Diversity Organizations:

- NMSDC (National Minority Supplier Diversity Council) and its Regional Councils [This organization is not open to non-minority women.] www.nmsdc.org
- WBENC (Women's Business Enterprise National Council) and its Regional Partners [This organization is for women owned businesses only] www.wbenc.org
- NAWBO (National Association of Women Business Owners) and its local Chapters [This organization is for women owned businesses only] www.nawbo.org
- NWBOC (National Women's Business Owners Corporation) [This organization is for women owned businesses only and provides certification and e-procurement services.] www.nwboc.org
- SBA (Small Business Associations) www.sba.gov. [Regional SBA Offices often hold events such as a Small Business Appreciation Banquet"; the corporate sponsors of and attendees to these events are potential Prospects.]

All of these organizations provide the names of their corporate members on their websites. Even if you do not qualify for membership or certification you can still use their corporate member list to find Prospects.

There are other organizations and membership-based exchanges whose primary function is to facilitate interaction between W/MBEs, Small or Disadvantaged businesses and the corporate, government and education entities that utilize Supplier Diversity. They may publish the names of their corporate members on their websites.

Also, remember government agencies and education institutions that are serious about Supplier Diversity often participate in these organizations.

Following is a course of action that will help you use these organizations to find and qualify Prospects:

Tasks
Look at the websites of the organizations listed and print their list of national corporate members. Save the website link on your computer. If possible save an electronic copy of the list.
Look at the websites of the local chapters of these organizations and print the list of their corporate members.
Conduct an Internet search to find Supplier Diversity organizations in your geographic area. If these organizations provide a list of their corporate members, print it.
Look closely at the lists and determine which ones are likely to use your products or services. Make a list of these.
Go back to the organizations website and look for indicators that your likely Prospect is truly involved in the organization (see previous bullets). Prioritize your list for further research based on the degree of participation by the corporate member.
Get on your regional SBA distribution list for announcements about events. If possible attend the events and make note of the corporate attendees. If you cannot attend, make note of the corporate sponsors.
Revisit the websites of the organizations at least every six months to see if there are new members or if your most likely Prospects have changed their degree of participation.

This Action is about identifying Prospects. It is important to remember there are many other factors involved in qualifying a Prospect. This Action is designed to provide you a tool to help you focus in on corporations (and others) who are serious about Supplier Diversity so that you will know if it is beneficial to use the angle that you are a Small Business, are owned by a Minority, Woman or Veteran or are a Disadvantaged Business.

Action #47

Take advantage of the fact that many major corporations who have Supplier Diversity Policies and/or Programs expect their major suppliers to also have policies.

A corporation with a Supplier Diversity Policy normally sets a goal for the amount of money they will spend with Small, Woman or Minority Owned, and Disadvantaged Businesses. If they are Prime Contractors to federal government entities they may also have goals for the amount of money to be spent with Veteran Owned or Service Disabled Veteran Owned Businesses. If they are doing any kind of government funded work they probably are required to set and meet these goals. The current tendency is for these Corporations to expect the companies in their Supply Chain – Suppliers/Vendors – to help them meet their goals by having policies and practices that are similar. They expect their Direct/Tier One and sometimes Second Level/Tier Two Suppliers to help them meet this goal.

The philosophy behind this is that every vendor/supplier from beginning to end will make an effort to include and encourage Supplier/Vendor Diversity.

Supply Chain

Any product or service has a Supply Chain. This chain is the system of businesses, organizations and people that participate in the manufacture and/or delivery of a product or service. Supply Chains are a little harder to clearly recognize for services than products, but the chain is there. Here are a few very basic examples:

Simple Supply Chain for a Desk

Tree Farmer grows and harvests oak trees	*There could be a supplier of seeds or saplings prior to this stage*
Trucking Company transports oak trees to Saw Mill	*Tree Farmer may do this or use a separate company; either way there are Suppliers to this stage: truck manufacturer and sales, fuel, tires, etc.*
Saw Mill turns the logs into boards	*There are Suppliers to the Saw Mill: saw manufacturer and sales, electricity, etc.*
Trucking Company transports boards to Furniture Plant	*Same scenario as the previous transport. The Trucking Company could be an individual who owns one rig.*
Furniture Plant builds desk	*In order to build the desk the Furniture Plant needs machinery, electricity, nails, glue, etc. They may use temporary staffing.*
Furniture Plant stains/paints/finishes the desk	*In order to complete the desk the Furniture Plant needs stain, paint, polyurethane, machinery, cloths, etc. The Furniture Manufacturer may outsource this function.*
Trucking Company transports desk to Office Furniture Store	*More transporting, may use the same Trucking Company or a different one.*

Office Furniture Store displays and sells desk	*The Office Furniture Store has its own Supply Chain; it probably gets the products it sells from multiple manufacturers. The Store also needs power, water, etc.*
Trucking Company transports desk to Purchaser in a box	*Sometimes the Furniture Store does the transporting itself, but still must purchase trucks, fuel, tires, etc.*
Subcontractor assembles desk at Purchaser's location	*Some Office Furniture Stores use Subcontractors to deliver and assemble furniture.*

There are obviously other products and services involved in this Supply Chain and those of the Suppliers/Vendors. Things like office supplies, safety equipment, legal and accounting services, etc. are necessary for the Furniture Manufacturer, Furniture Store and others to operate. The right column gives you some idea of places a small business could insert itself. If the office desk manufacturer expects its Suppliers/Vendors to practice Supplier Diversity then a Small, Minority/Woman/Veteran Owned or Disadvantaged Business increases its chances of being the chosen Subcontractor at the points mentioned in the right column. It will take some understanding of a Supply Chain in to find the opportunities to effectively propose your business as a link in the chain.

Simple Supply Chain for Facility Maintenance

Manufacturer contracts with a company to provide complete Facility Maintenance	*Depending on the size of the manufacturing facility the Facility Maintenance company that gets the contract could be a Diverse Supplier.*
Facility Maintenance Company purchases cleaning supplies and materials	*A business will need to provide the cleaning supplies and materials. The Facility Maintenance Company could also choose to Subcontract the cleaning completely.*
Facility Maintenance Company purchases materials, tools and equipment to maintain and repair the building(s)	*Again the materials would need to be purchased, but a Subcontractor could be used to provide the maintenance services completely.*
Specific, occasional services such as Heating/Air Conditioning, Electrical, Telecommunications and Plumbing	*The Facility Maintenance Company may have people on staff to do these things, but is more likely to outsource/subcontract them. Either way the supplies to do this work must be purchased and delivered.*
Sometimes security is included in a Facility Maintenance contract	*This is a service that is often outsourced. Uniforms and other supplies and equipment are needed.*
Landscape services are often included in a Facility Maintenance contract	*This is another service that is likely to be outsourced. Lawn equipment, fuel, fencing, seeds, plants, sand, mulch, etc., etc. are needed for landscaping.*

Seasonal or occasional things, such production line semi-annual preventive maintenance or installation of holiday decorations, may require temporary workers	*A Temporary Staffing company is the most likely Subcontractor for this service; however, if it is something like the installation of holiday decorations a company that does that kind of work may be hired.*

Again there are other products and services required to provide Facility Maintenance. Some large businesses will include any money spent with Diverse suppliers/vendors to count toward the Supplier Diversity goal, but others only include products and services directly related to the contract service. If only the direct suppliers are included then money spent on things such as office supplies, accounting services, marketing, HR Services, etc. will not be counted.

Your best opportunities may be with the Direct/Tier One or Second Level/Tier Two Suppliers. It is important to identify which corporations have Supplier Diversity Policies and conduct research to discover their Suppliers. Typically these Tier One and Two businesses are in a better position to utilize your products and services than the larger corporation. Often the large corporation will have a person or staff designated to facilitate and encourage the use of Small, Woman/Minority/Veteran Owned and Disadvantaged Businesses. This person can likely assist you in identifying and contacting the Direct/Tier One and Second Level/Two Suppliers and may be willing to make the introduction.

Action #48

Identify professional organizations that your Prospects participate in and find ways to benefit from observing and/or participating.

You should conduct research to find out if there is a professional organization for the specific industries/business types or functions (such as City Management or City Council) that are good Prospects for your products and services. Most industries and functions do have a professional organization.

Here are just a few industries/business types or functions that have professional organizations:

- Architecture
- Decorating
- Event Planning/Management
- Construction (including specific areas such as electrical, or classifications such as the National Association of Women In Construction [NAWIC])
- Food Service
- Accounting
- Legal
- Banking
- Insurance
- Teaching
- Real Estate
- Manufacturing (there are general manufacturing organizations, organizations for specific functions within manufacturing (i.e. Supply Chain Management), and there are organizations for particular types of manufacturing (i.e. automotive)
- Facilities/Property Management
- School Boards
- School Management (Supervisors, Principals, etc.)
- Municipalities (elected and staff)
- Counties (elected and staff)
- Nursing
- Hospital/Medical Facility Management
- Employment
- Non-Profit Management
- Chambers of Commerce (both as a general business organization and because they often have specialized groups (i.e. manufacturing or retail)

When you identify a professional organization that serves your Prospects you need to look for ways that observation and/or participation can benefit you. Following are some examples:

WAYS TO PARTICIPATE	BENEFIT QUESTIONS	CAUTIONS
Membership	Will this enhance your reputation because you are accepted by or supportive of the organization? Will it provide access to other members that are Prospects for your business?	Many professional organizations do not allow you to be a member unless you are actually in the profession or perform the function. For example if you do not have a Realtors license you cannot join the local Board of Realtors. However, many professional organizations do allow affiliate memberships for those who work with or sell to the real members. An affiliate membership may be beneficial, just be clear on the privileges and benefits of this type of

WAYS TO PARTICIPATE	BENEFIT QUESTIONS	CAUTIONS
		membership.
Member List	At the conference can you verify that your Prospects are members? Can you obtain Prospect contact information that you do not already have?	Can you get this information without paying to join this organization.
Meeting Attendance	Will attending the meetings provide you access to members and knowledge of their needs?	Do you have to join to attend the meetings? Can you attend occasional meetings without joining?
Conference Attendance	Can you attend the same meetings, events as the members? Will you get opportunities to learn about the needs, problems, trends and issues of your Prospects? Will you get direct access to the members?	When determining the cost of attending be sure to include all expenses and take your time into consideration?
Vendor Booth at Conference or Event	See page 148 in the Chapter on Trade Fairs & Networking Events for more advice.	When determining the cost of a booth, be sure to include all expenses and take your time into

WAYS TO PARTICIPATE	BENEFIT QUESTIONS	CAUTIONS
		consideration?
Presenter at Conference	See page 148 in the Chapter on Trade Fairs & Networking Events for more advice.	When deciding if this is beneficial be sure to calculate the cost including all expenses – travel, handouts, preparation time.
Sponsor of Conference, Event or Session	See page 148 in the Chapter on Trade Fairs & Networking Events for more advice.	If you do decide this is worth the cost be sure you do everything possible to capitalize on it. I've seen companies sponsor something and then waste the opportunity by not even attending.
Newsletter	Will the membership classification available to you include a subscription to the organization's newsletter or other publications? Publications can provide information on issues, trends,	Can you get the newsletter without the cost of joining?

WAYS TO PARTICIPATE	BENEFIT QUESTIONS	CAUTIONS
	needs, regulations, etc. that you can use to show the benefits and applicability of your products/services.	
Information	Will observing the organization, it's website, it's press releases, etc. provide insight on the members (your Prospects) needs?	If the information does not come to you via member notices, newsletters, etc. then you will have to regularly visit their website and/or watch the media.
Speaker	Does the organization use speakers at their meetings or events? Often they have difficulty finding speakers.	At lot of times organizations allow vendors to speak at their meetings, but do not allow them to use the opportunity to make a "sells pitch". Even if you cannot sell, you may be able to educate, and in the long run influence their purchasing.

It sounds as if this Action will take a lot of time, but it is not as complicated or time consuming as it seems. Consider it preparation for focused marketing efforts. It is also worth the effort and time because well-prepared for focused marketing saves money and gets better results.

Some places and ways to find professionals organizations:

- Internet searches
- Library
- Walls of your clients/customers offices (they often display membership plaques)
- Local newspapers (meetings are often published in calendars)

Chapter 5
GETTING THE WORD OUT/
GETTING NOTICED

Action #49

Develop, categorize and maintain an email Distribution List.

In order to get announcements, promotions or any marketing message out to the right people in a timely manner you need a well-maintained email Distribution List. Do not risk irritating people by sending them information they do not care about. In order to send information to the appropriate people it is important to categorize your list; this will also make distribution of information more efficient.

Here are some tips to help with this tedious, but vital Action:

- Dedicate a specific amount of time each month (or week or quarter) to be spent on developing and maintaining a Distribution List
- Determine classifications to use in distributing information. Example classifications:
    - Current Clients/Customers
    - Past Clients/Customers
    - Qualified Prospects
    - Professional Organizations
    - Media

- Determine a format for the Distribution List (i.e. Customer Management Software, Excel Spread Sheet, Table in Word document, Access, etc.).
- Develop a standard phrase to be added to any email that states why they are receiving it and that if they would like to opt out how they should do it. This is a legal requirement to combat Spam. Here is an example of one:
  You are receiving this email because you previously signed up for our Distribution List. If you would like to discontinue receiving emails, please respond to this email with **Unsubscribe** *in the Subject line.*
- Always update the list when bounce back and undeliverable emails are received.
- Whenever you encounter a person (request for information phone call, meeting, conference, etc.) ask if they would like to be added to your Distribution List.
- Develop a schedule for maintaining your Distribution List.

Action #50

Include your Small, Disadvantaged or Ownership status on your business cards.

If you have any Certifications – Woman/Minority/Veteran Owned, DBE (Disadvantaged Business Enterprise), etc. – include them on your business card. The SBA (Small Business Administration) does not certify businesses as Small Business, but if you meet the guidelines then you can make that claim; visit this page on the SBA website to determine if you meet the requirements to be officially classified as a Small Business http://web.sba.gov/faqs/faqindex.cfm?areaID=15. If you have multiple Certifications or if you have permission to use the logo you may want to put them on the back.

Action #51

<u>Include your Small Business status or Disadvantaged or Minority/Woman/Veteran Owned Certifications on your brochures and other marketing materials.</u>

This is a subtle way for you to let people know that you are certified as Minority/Woman/Veteran Owned, Disadvantaged or classified as a Small Business. You can state it in the text of your brochure, list it on the back, include it as footer; whatever seems appropriate for your business and the intended recipient of the brochure or material. Remember that having one or more of these classifications is one of your marketing angles, not the basis for your marketing effort and certainly not the foundation of your business. It does need to be included, but it should not be featured.

On the following page is a checklist to be sure you have included it in the important places.

Including Small, Ownership or Disadvantaged status in or on these items depends on how many of your Customers/Clients and Prospects care about your Small/Disadvantaged classification or Ownership status. You may even want to have two versions of some things – one *with* for those who care and one *without* for those who don't.

Included (/)	Marketing Material or Place
	Stationery
	Envelopes *
	Labels *
	Brochures
	Electronic Brochure
	Business Card
	Flyers
	One-Pager
	Website
	Appointment Cards
	Post Cards
	Email Signature (information that is inserted at the bottom of all your emails)*
	Your Office or Waiting Room (display your certificate)
	Printed promotional items (such as bookmarks, pens, magnets, etc)
	Mail Outs
	"About" information in press releases
	Advertisements
	Blog
	Newsletter
	Exhibit Material (signs, table covers, etc.)*

Action #52

Announce new Certifications to those who care.

If you have recently been Certified or renewed a Certification as a Minority, Woman or Veteran Owned Business it is acceptable and advantageous to announce it. Just be careful that you only announce it to people who care. If you make it a big deal to those who do not care, you run the risk of a negative reaction because it is perceived as entitlement or that you rely on getting business through your ownership status. Guidance on determining who cares if you are Certified is provided in this book on page 14.

One of the best ways to make your Certification announcement is through a press release. The release can, of course, be sent to the media, but it can also be used in the following ways:

- Posted on media websites that allow reader postings. (Most newspapers pull some self-posted releases and use them in the printed paper so this method increases your possibilities for publication.)
- Mailed or emailed to those on your distribution list that care
- Posted on your website
- Posted on social media sites with a link to your website
- Handed out at Trade Fairs and Conferences

On the following page is example text for a press release. You can add other details that enhance the message. You could also add a quote from the business owner or appropriate staff member, such as "*We are pleased to achieve this certification because it will help our government clients achieve their goals for doing business with Small Businesses.* Just remember that you stand a better chance of getting it published and read if it is brief.

Example press release:

Shannon Services, LLC has been certified as a Minority Owned Business by the State of _____.*

This Certification is awarded to businesses that are owned and managed by a minority or woman. The State* provides this Certification to facilitate the use of Minority Owned Businesses in state procurement**.

Shannon Services, LLC is a Happy City business that provides _____. The company recently celebrated its third year in business.

Additional information on Shannon Services, LLC is available on the company website at www._____. State Certification information can be found on the State website at www._____.

---

* The exact name (and acronym) of the agency or organization providing the Certification should be used in the announcement.

** The entities (state agencies, corporations, etc.) served by the Certifying agency or organization should be used in the announcement.

Action #53

Register on CCR (Central Contractor Registration). If you are already registered be sure your information is current. *(CCR is always updating and revamping so you want to be sure your information is correct and comprehensive and that you are using this important database to your best advantage.)*

CCR www.ccr.gov is the primary registrant database for the Federal Government and its Prime Contractors. CCR not only collects and stores information for use by Federal purchasers and Federal Prime Contractors; it also validates information. Your business must be registered in this database before you can be awarded any type of Federal contract or agreement or before a Federal Prime Contractor can use your business as a Subcontractor. (Actually a Prime Contractor can use any Subcontractor they choose, but if that Subcontractor is not registered on CCR the Prime will not get credit toward their mandatory goals for the use of Small, Minority/Woman/Veteran Owned or Disadvantaged Businesses. Because of this you will likely not even be considered if you are not registered in CCR.)

Before you register you will need a DUNS number (see previous Action on page 13) and a Federal Tax ID (see Action on page 10) in order to register. You will also need to know the NAICS Codes that apply to your business (see previous Action on page 11). It is important to complete this registration accurately because it will provide information on your business to Prospects. You do not have to complete the registration in one session, but remember that you are not actually registered until you have completed the on-line form. You may find it helpful to begin the registration and find out what type of information you will need, then save the form and return when you have collected everything you need.

Assistance in completing the online CCR registration is provided by some PTACs (Procurement Technical Assistance Centers). PTACs are a resource offered by the Department of Defense to provide at no or minimal cost assistance to businesses in marketing to the federal, state and local government entities. The resource is available to any business, not just those seeking to do business with the Department of Defense. For a list of the PTACs by state visit this website http://www.dla.mil/db/procurem.htm.

Action #54

Register as a Vendor with your County government

County governments need/use numerous and varied products and services. Some of them list on their websites many of the products and services they use on a regular basis; but it would be impossible for them to list everything, especially things rarely used. So do not assume that they do not use the products or services you provide. You need to register in order to receive notification of opportunities to bid or propose. A county will likely label their list of people to receive notifications one of the following:

- Vendor List or Vendor Database
- Bidder List or Bidder Database
- Purchasing or Procurement Database

Counties will normally use one of these registration methods:

- Online registration form
- Online form that can be printed, completed and mailed or faxed to the County
- No formal registration, you must send a letter requesting to be on the Vendor/Bidder List. (An Action on page 66 assists you with this.)

It is important to remember that registering as a Vendor/Bidder is totally separate from being Certified. Registration is usually done with a Purchasing/Procurement Department or Office and Certification is not normally part of that Department. Never assume that because you are <u>Certified</u> by any government or education entity that you are also <u>registered</u> with any entity or business. The registration form will likely include blanks for information on your Small, Disadvantaged or Minority/Woman/Veteran Owned status and Certifications. However, there may be a separate/additional form to register as a Disadvantaged or Minority/Woman/Veteran Owned Business. If there is a separate form from the general vendor/supplier registration form you will need to complete both. If the County does not include a way for you to provide this information you will need to dig deeper and determine if they have a Supplier/Vendor Diversity or Minority/Woman Owned Business Use Policy. If they do not and they are a good Prospect for you, then you will want to use other marketing angles than your Small, Disadvantaged or Ownership status.

Following is a list of the typical things requested in an online registration:

- Business Name
- Business Address
- Contact Name, Email, Title, Phone Number
- Owner(s) Name(s)
- Type of Business (Corporation, Partnership, LLC, etc.)
- Tax ID Number or Social Security Number if Sole Proprietor/Self Employed
- Website
- Shipping Address
- Payment Address (if different from Mailing Address)
- NIGP Codes (See page 12 of this book for explanation)
- Diversity Status (Small, Disadvantaged, Minority-Owned, Woman-Owned, Veteran-Owned, etc.) – you may have to supply proof of certification by downloading or mailing a copy of your certificate
- Terms (Due on receipt, net 30 days, etc)
- Years in business
- If you use electronic billing and payment receipt
- Your business or operation license number (if a license is required by the county)
- References (related to local government if you have them) – include contact information, preferably an email address

On the following page is a form that you can use to make a list of this information so that you have it handy when you start the registration process.

Name	
Address	
Contact Name & Title	
Contact Email	
Contact Phone Number	
Owner(s) Name(s)	
Type of Business	
Tax ID/SS Number	
Website	
Shipping Address	
Payment Address	
NIGP Codes	
Diversity Certifications	
Terms	
Years in Business	
Business License (place & number)	
Reference 1	
Reference 2	

Reference 3	

Action #55

<u>Determine which departments or offices in your county government need your products and services.</u>

Most departments within a county government make their own purchasing decisions or, at least, develop the specifications and evaluation criteria. You need to know who needs your products and services so that you can conduct research and develop a marketing strategy to build a relationship with the people in that department. Knowing the function of a department or office is the first key in determining if they need your product or service. For instance: if you provide landscaping services then the departments most likely to need your services are the departments that deal with one or more of the following: parks, streets or utilities. If you provide IT (Information Technology) services or products then the IT Department is your most likely candidate because Counties tend to centralize IT functions, applications, services and equipment into one department; however, there may be departments that have complete responsibility and therefore purchasing power for specific IT applications or equipment. Some possibilities for these specific applications or equipment are Economic Development, GIS (Geographic Information System), Emergency Services (911 and Dispatch) or Health Department.

The research will also tell you if being Small, Disadvantaged or Minority/Woman/Veteran Owned is a useful marketing angle. Once you have determined which departments in your county government need your services you will be able to apply that knowledge to other counties. The current trend is that counties are less likely to have strong Vendor Diversity policies and programs than cities.

Use the space in the following form to list the most likely departments/offices and set a target date to contact them. Be sure you register as a vendor with the county as a whole before making contact with the individual departments – protocol is important.

Departments/Offices to contact in _____County

Department/Office	Need	Need is Identified (I) or Likely (L)	Target Contact Date

Action #56

Make a list of the counties in the first hundred miles of your geographic circle (the geographic area you can profitably serve) and develop a schedule for registering in their database.

Registering in your home county is great. But if you can provide your products and services in other counties, it is even more important to let them know you exist. This is because you are more reliant on them alerting you to opportunities since you are not as likely to be aware of the opportunities through posted notices and media coverage. Registration in their vendor/bidder database is critical to having them know about your company. It is fine to register with counties farther than 100 miles away from you if you can feasibly provide products/services in those counties. However, you need to start somewhere so draw a circle around your location that is 100 miles from you at any point then register with the counties in that area. If 100 miles is too far for you, then set your own distance. Do not worry about state lines because often a Prospect in another state is just as good as one in your state if the other more important factors line up – proximity, need of the Prospect, your ability to provide, etc.

Make your list, set target dates and record your completion in the following form. You can use the information you recorded in the table on page 110 to complete the registrations.

COUNTY	TARGET DATE TO REGISTER	ACTUAL DATE REGISTERED

Action #57

Establish a schedule to complete the departmental list on each of the counties in the previous list.

Use the form on page 112 to make your departmental list for each county. Each time you make a departmental list it will be easier and take less time because you will learn from each list you make. Following is a form to help you establish this schedule.

COUNTY	TARGET DATE TO COMPLETE DEPARTMENT LIST	TARGET DATE DEPARTMENT LIST COMPLETED

Action #58

Register as a Vendor with the city where your business is located (or is near)

Many municipalities (cities, towns, villages, townships, districts, etc) have databases of Vendors/Bidders similar to Counties. It is important to understand that counties and municipalities are usually completely separate and being registered with one does not mean you are registered with others. For example: being registered with Larimer County in Colorado does not mean that you are registered with each (or any) of the cities or towns in that County. The information provided in the previous Actions about registering with a county (beginning on page 108) also applies to this Action. You can use the information you filled in the table for that Action to register in your local city/town.

Action #59

Determine which department or departments in your city government need your products and services.

This Action is just like previous Action #55 about county government departments but this time for cities and towns in the geographic area you can profitably serve. Remember that county governments and city governments do not necessarily have the same departments because they do not always provide the same services or do the same functions. For example a city is more likely to provide a waste (trash) pick up service; a county is more likely to have a roads and bridges operation. Use the following form to accomplish this Action.

Departments/Offices to contact in _____City

Department/Office	Need	Need is Identified (I) or Likely (L)	Target Contact Date

Action #60

Make a list of appropriate cities in the first hundred miles of your geographic circle (the geographic area you can profitably serve) and develop a schedule for registering in their database.

It is important to register in the city nearest you. It is also important to register with other cities in the area you can serve. Starting with the same geographical circle that you are using for counties will be more efficient because of the following:

- It is easier to keep records if the geographic circle is the same.
- In some counties the county government and the municipal government of the county seat have merged (note: sometimes you still must register with both if you are Small, Disadvantaged or Woman/Minority/Veteran Owned).
- If you decide that in-person visits are appropriate then those visits will be more easily accomplished if you can schedule several cities and a county for a single trip.

Establish your criteria for an appropriate city/town. Here are some possibilities:

- Population
- Geographic size
- Departments (If you provide a product/service used by police departments and the town does not have a police department then, obviously, it is not a real Prospect. Never assume a city/town has a department/office/function or you will waste time and risk reputation by offering them a product/service they do not need.)
- Need
- Budget (If you read in the news that the city/town is operating in the red and your product/service is not required by law, it might not be the time to make contact)
- Laws (local, state, federal)

Make your list, set target dates and record your completion in the following form:

CITY/TOWN	TARGET DATE TO REGISTER	ACTUAL DATE REGISTERED

Action #61

Establish a schedule to complete the departmental list on each of the cities/towns in the previous list.

Use the form on page 116 to make your departmental list for each city/town. Each time you make a departmental list it will be easier and take less time because you will learn from each list you make. Following is a form to help you establish this schedule.

CITY/TOWN	TARGET DATE TO COMPLETE DEPARTMENT LIST	TARGET DATE DEPARTMENT LIST COMPLETED

Action #62

Examine the utility providers in your area to see if they are likely Prospects.

Utility providers may be private businesses, part of another government entity or a cooperative. All of them must adhere to specific regulations. The ones that are part of a government entity (city or county) are subject to that entity's procurement and Supplier Diversity rules. The private businesses and cooperatives set their own policies about Supplier Diversity, but may have to comply with the Subcontracting Supplier Diversity policies of their customers if they have government contracts. A public utility may be loosely associated with a government entity (city or county) but have its own governing board/committee and, therefore, have its own procurement and Supplier Diversity rules; these utilities often have "Public Works" in their name.

These utility entities are likely to offer at least one of the following in a specified geographic area:

- Electricity
- Water
- Sewer
- Telecommunications/Data Communications
- Cable Television

The first step is identifying the utility providers in your area. The next step is to determine if the utility provider(s) needs your products or services. Keep in mind that utility providers use a lot of products and services, so even if you do not sell pipe, wire or safety gear or provide trenching services, there may still be opportunities for you. Many times utility providers use a company to completely handle a large project and expect that Prime Contractor to use Small, Disadvantaged or M/WBEs as Subcontractors. Chances are if one utility provider has need of your products and service, then so will others.

To make your research and contacting efforts efficient coordinate with your research, registration and contact plans for counties and cities as outlined in this chapter. This is suggested because the utility may be part of the city or county or it likely uses similar geographic boundaries. If you follow this suggested coordination then you will be first researching and contacting those in a 100 mile radius of your location. Use the following form to list the Utilities as you identify them. If the Utility is part of another government entity and uses that entity's database, then make note of that in this form so that you do not have to back track to be sure that you have registered. The contact target date should still be set because it is important to contact the Utility directly.

Use the following form to accomplish this Action:

Utility	Target Register Date	Actual Register Date	Target Contact Date	Actual Contact Date

Action #63

Register as a Vendor with the School District nearest your business

Often School Districts are separate from a County or Municipality (city/town) and have their own purchasing/procurement process and staff. That means it is necessary to register as a Vendor/Bidder with each School District. Some counties have multiple School Districts so be sure you register with each of them. Very often School Districts must follow the procurement laws of its State and normally State procurement laws include a Vendor Diversity or Minority/Woman Business Use Policy. So, even though the School District may not have a registration form or publicized policy it is likely that it is important to them if you are Small, Disadvantaged or Minority/Woman Owned because it is important in the State Procurement laws. It is worth mentioning even if there is not a blank on the registration form. If the registration is done online and there is no place to state that you are Small, Disadvantaged or Minority/Woman/Veteran Owned, you will need to find a subtle way, that does not make it appear that you have a feeling of entitlement, to get the information in front of the right people. Some ideas are suggested in Actions later in this book.

The likely information required in a vendor registration for counties provided in the Action on page 109 is basically the same for School Districts.

Use the table below to list the School Districts in the home county of your business and set target dates for registration.

SCHOOL DISTRICT	TARGET DATE TO REGISTER	ACTUAL DATE REGISTERED

Action #64

<u>Identify departments, offices and initiatives in the School Districts nearest you that are likely to use your products or services.</u>

Sometimes the products or services you offer are best sold directly to schools, but School Districts normally have explicit procurement/purchasing regulations that include what an individual school can purchase on their own and what must go through a department or office at the district level. The primary reason for this is to get quantity discounts. If you break protocol and contact a school directly when the regulations state that a department or office has purchasing jurisdiction, then you will at best taint your reputation and at worst lose the opportunity and possibly future opportunities.

Here are some suggestions to guide your research and thought process:

- If you offer a product that can be sold as a fund raiser then follow this sequence
    o Register in the vendor database as detailed in the Action above
    o Contact the Purchasing/Procurement Office or person and ask them what the rules are for contacting schools about your product; ask if there are any restrictions or dates that apply.
    o Follow the rules
    o Keep a record of the schools as you make contact; include the reaction and note if they already use a fund raising product
- If you offer an education software product then find the department or office that makes decisions and sets policy on education software. After you have registered in the vendor database, make contact with this department or office. Some possibilities for the department/office responsible for education software are:
    o Grade Level (i.e. Elementary, Middle, High School)

- o Curriculum
- o Instructional
- o Technology
- If you offer janitorial services or supplies it will probably be best to contact a District department instead of a specific school because the District will likely see this as a place where they can cut costs be getting quantity discounts. Probable department names are:
  - o Facilities
  - o Buildings
  - o Operations
  - o Engineering

Use this table to list the School District Departments or Schools you need to contact and set target dates:

School District	Department, Office, Initiative or School	Target Contact Date	Actual Contact Date

Action #65

Make a list of the school districts in the first hundred miles of your geographic circle (the geographic area you can profitably serve) and develop a schedule for registering in their database.

As is true with counties and cities/towns you are more reliant on a school district alerting you to opportunities since you are not as likely to be aware of the opportunities through posted notices and media coverage. Registration in the district's vendor/bidder database is critical to having them know about your company. if you can profitably serve school districts farther than 100 miles away from you then should register in those counties. However, starting with the first100 mile circle around you allows you to coordinate with your efforts with the counties, cities/towns and utilities in that area. Set your own geographical circle if 100 miles is too far for you. As with local governments do not be afraid to cross state lines since a Prospect in another state may be as feasible as those in your home state.

Make your list, set target dates and record your completion in the following form. You can use the information you recorded in the table on page 110 to register.

SCHOOL DISTRICT	TARGET DATE TO REGISTER	ACTUAL DATE REGISTERED

Action #66

Establish a schedule to complete the departmental list on each of the school districts in the previous list.

Use the form on page 124 to make your departmental list for each school district. Each time you make a departmental list it will be easier and take less time because you will learn from each list you make. Following is a form to help you establish this schedule.

SCHOOL DISTRICT	TARGET DATE TO COMPLETE DEPARTMENT LIST	TARGET DATE DEPARTMENT LIST COMPLETED

Action #67

Register as a vendor with your home State.

The list and diversity of products and services used by the agencies, departments and other entities of a State is even greater than that of counties and cities. Even if you determined that the State Capital is not in your profitable geographic area (refer to the Action on page 55), remember that there probably are agency, department, school, office locations in your profitable geographic area. Most States use online registration and if so this will be the only method for registering as a potential vendor. Being certified by a State or by a State Department of Transportation (DOT) does not mean that you are registered as a potential vendor; Certification and registration are two separate things. Some certification applications do include information that will be used to automatically register you as a potential vendor, but do not assume this is the case.

Here are a few facts that will help you get registered:

- Vendor registration is usually part of the procurement/purchasing process and done by the department that handles that process.
- Some states separate the procurement of technology services and products from the procurement of all other services and products.

- Vendor registration likely will require you to include NAICS codes (see page 11 for explanation and information on these codes). Some states include a list of products and services in their online registration and you are asked to *check* the ones you provide.
- The vendor registration form will probably include questions/blanks associated with being a Small, Disadvantaged or Minority/Woman/Veteran Owned Business
- You are responsible for keeping the information up to date.

Use the following form to make note of information you will need to register as a vendor with your State.

Company Name	
Tax Identification (EIN or Social Security)	
State Tax ID	
Contact Name	
Contact Phone	
Contact Email	
Mailing Address	
Order Address	
Payment Address	
Secondary Contact Name	
Secondary Contact Phone	
Secondary Contact Email	

Business Description	
Website (URL)	
Certifications	
Licenses	

Remember that registration is not the end; it is the beginning. You have to be on the list, but being on the list is not enough. You must introduce your company, build relationships and stay in front of the right people. Other Actions in this book will help you with that.

Actions #68 & #69

Following are two Actions that work together to help you sell your products and services to State Departments of Transportation.

Register as a Vendor with your State Department of Transportation (DOT)

Apply for Certification as a DBE (Disadvantaged Business Enterprise) by your State DOT

When it comes to purchasing, in most states the Department of Transportation operates separately from other state agencies and departments. This agency is a hybrid of state and federal money, state and federal projects, state and federal requirements, state and federal laws. The state DOTs try to bring everything under one umbrella, but merging funding, rules and requirements can be complicated and tricky. This means that state DOTs probably have their own:

- Purchasing Department
- Certification for disadvantaged businesses
- Project Managers
- Funding/Financial Staff
- Board or Commission

Most state DOTs maintain one vendor database and administer their own certification program. Because they receive federal funds for many, if not most, of their roads and bridges projects they must follow Federal DOT guidelines for the use of Disadvantaged Businesses. Therefore most state DOTs have a staff to certify, train and facilitate the involvement of DBEs (Disadvantaged Business Enterprises) in federal funded projects. The requirements for being certified as a DBE are normally outlined very clearly on the website of the state DOT under the "Doing Business With" section. This section also explains how to register in the vendor database. It is important to remember that certification and vendor registration are two separate functions and that's why this book lists them as two separate Actions.

Projects and functions that are paid for with state funds do not have to follow the Federal guidelines and requirements for the use of DBEs. Instead the procurement rules for state agencies and departments usually apply, including the use of Small, Minority/Woman Owned or Disadvantaged Businesses.

In case you are thinking that DOT is not a likely Prospect for you, don't rule them out until you have talked with them. They are a huge department and therefore include many functions and needs. Here are a few examples:

- Safety products (vests, glasses, flags, cones, etc.)
- Buildings (construction and maintenance)
- Landscaping (around buildings, along roads)
- IT Services and Products
- Training
- Temporary Staffing
- Public/Community Relations

- Design Services
- Event Planning and Coordination
- Printing

The information required in the vendor registration is usually pretty much the same as that of the regular state vendor registration. That information is detailed in the previous Action on page 128.

Even though the DOT's staffs try to shield their vendors and the public from the complications of being a hybrid, it can be very advantageous for a vendor to understand the specifics of the funding, rules and requirements. A little research can go a long way toward getting business with this agency.

Action #70

Register as a vendor with the state supported university or college nearest you.

State supported universities and colleges (including community and technical) normally are required to follow state procurement/purchasing laws; which means they are probably required to have goals for the percentage of money they will spend with Small/Disadvantaged Businesses and M/WBEs. The education institutions usually do their own purchasing of goods and services and maintain their own databases of vendors. The information you will need to register is basically the same information required to register as a vendor with your State.

Remember that even though being in the vendor/supplier database (on the list) of a college or university is probably necessary, it is not enough. You will still need to develop a relationship with the purchasers and users of your products and services.

Action #71

Identify and contact the appropriate departments, schools, institutions, foundations, initiatives or other entities within the university or college nearest you.

Universities and colleges can be very complex communities with many areas of control and responsibility. It was suggested in a previous Action that you register in the individual university or college vendor database because that is the necessary first step. However, because of the distributed control and responsibility you must zero in on those most likely to use your products or services and make your business known to them. Some of the factors to consider are:

- If the university/college is state supported it must follow state procurement codes/laws
- Within a university/college there can be a foundation, institution or other entity that is somewhat separate from the university/college and therefore, not subject to the state procurement codes/laws
- The division of control and responsibility is not the same in all universities/colleges, not even in a single state
- Funding sources (state, federal, local, private, grants) may drive some of the purchasing practices and rules

Hopefully, this list helps you understand that it is important to do research and understand how you can fit into this complex community.

It is easy get to get lost on a college campus if you are not familiar with it. All the buildings are named after people and do not necessarily identify themselves by function or tenant. Roads end abruptly or go in a loop without warning. Parking is limited and the parking areas are covered with signs that scream "Reserved for Faculty." Students on foot and bicycles have the right of way and will cross in front of you without looking both ways. You can normally pick up a campus map at the Visitors Center. Studying this map before you start on your journey will help you find your way. However, all the dead end roads and other surprises will not be identified. But ask any Freshman, once you become familiar with the campus you can find your way around easily and you will know the shortcuts and the obstacles. This physical example is a good illustration of the non-physical structure of a university/college. Both evolved over time so any map or master plan is a rough sketch. But with research and perseverance you can learn the structure and make it work to your advantage. One reason to do this is that very few vendors make the effort – that sets you apart and gives you a competitive advantage.

Now, the best place to get your "map" for the procurement/purchasing journey is at the Vendor's "visitor's center" otherwise known as the Procurement or Purchasing Office/Department. This Office/Department will be glad to help you understand the rules and also give you information on the specific department, foundation, office, etc. that you should contact.

One other comforting thought. Even though each university/college is different, the things you learn from one can help you speed up the learning process at the next one.

Action #72

<u>Find out where your government and education prospects post their bidding opportunities and monitor the postings.</u>

Each government and education entity must advertise many of their bid and proposal opportunities. Typically they must post any purchase or project over $10,000. The specific type of purchases, where and how long they must be posted and other parameters are determined by the laws or rules of the government/education entity. Remember that all bid and proposal requests will not be posted. It is still important to establish and maintain a relationship with the appropriate staff at government and education entities so you will know about bid and proposal requests that do not have to be posted and so that you will have a better chance of knowing when an opportunity is coming before it is actually posted.

Knowing the rules and the places of postings are two reasons that it is so important to be familiar with your Prospects, Customer and Clients.

The following table provides you some common places that government entities will post their bid and proposal requests.

Government or Education Entity	Common Places Bid & Proposal Requests Will or May Be Posted
Federal Government Agencies, Departments & Offices	FedBizOpps at www.fbo.gov; website of each individual agency, department; newspapers; Subcontracting opportunities may be posted by Prime Contractors at http://web.sba.gov/subnet (more information on Subcontracting on page 82)
State Government Agencies, Departments & Offices	State purchasing website; website of each individual agency, department or office; newspapers; Subcontracting opportunities may also be posted on the websites of Prime Contractors.
State supported Colleges & Universities	State purchasing website; website of each individual college or university; newspapers; Subcontracting opportunities may also be posted on the websites of Prime Contractors.
Local Governments (cities, towns, counties, government utilities, etc.)	Website of the local government entity; newspapers; State government's purchasing website or newsletter.

Government or Education Entity	Common Places Bid & Proposal Requests Will or May Be Posted
School Districts	Website of the school district; newspapers; State government's purchasing website or newsletter.

Note: Often you can sign up on the posting websites or with Purchasing/Procurement departments to receive notices of bids in your classification.

Author's note:

Here is a piece of advice based on my 30+ years of working on all sides of government purchasing (selling, buying, advising, and analyzing). If you only respond to bid or proposal requests and never do the work necessary to know your government/education Prospects and establish and nurture a relationship with the people involved you will not be very successful at getting government/education business.

It is important to establish a schedule to monitor the websites for opportunities and also to follow buying trends. The trends you will see can help you keep your Marketing Plan relevant and realistic.

Action #73

Choose five of the most likely business/corporate Prospects for your products and services in your profitable geographic area and register in their database.

Almost all businesses/corporations use an online vendor registration. Also, most of them follow a similar protocol/process in considering Small Businesses of any type as potential vendors. Registering in the online database is normally the first step in the process to be considered as a potential vendor. So, do not jeopardize your opportunities by not following the normal protocol – complete the online vendor registration before making any contact with the business/corporation.

If you meet a purchaser or Supplier Diversity coordinator at some type of event and they say to send them some information, then do so after you complete the online registration. Chances are extremely high that they will direct you to complete that online registration at some point. They may suggest, when they first meet you at an event that you do the online registration and then contact them. Either way do the online registration first; you will impress them if you do because it shows both that you took the time to find out how they like to do business and that you care enough to follow their protocol.

The information requested in the online registration varies somewhat from one business to another because what they need to know when considering you as a vendor varies depending on their needs and business practices. However, the information on other vendor registrations provided in this chapter are good guides for getting started in compiling the information. Remember that the information requested is important to your Prospect, even if you do not understand why they ask for it.

Use the table on the following page to establish a time line for registering with these first five business/corporate Prospects.

Business/ Corporation	Date to Visit Website & Print form/directions	Date to finish compiling info for registration	Date to complete online registration

Actions #74 & #75

The following two Actions are covered together because the second is dependent on the purpose for the first.

Once you have completed the online vendor registration for five Prospects in your profitable geographic area contact the Supplier Diversity coordinator or the Purchasing Department.

Contact the designated Buyer for your products/services at your five Prospects.

If a business/corporation has a Supplier Diversity coordinator they normally would like to hear from you if you are officially a

Small, Minority/Woman/Veteran Owned or Disadvantaged Business. This is because it is their job to find qualified vendors that fit into these classifications. The Supplier Diversity contact will likely have one of the following titles:

- Supplier Diversity Coordinator or Director
- Vendor Diversity Coordinator or Director
- Small Business Liaison
- Small Business M/WBE Liaison
- M/WBE Coordinator

If there is not a designated Supplier Diversity contact then it is still advisable to contact the Purchasing Department. You can probably identify the specific buyer of your products/services through the website or a phone call to the Purchasing Department.

Usually the best way to make initial contact with the Supplier Diversity contact or Purchasing Department is to send an email with the electronic version of your one-pager.

Following is an example text for that email.

Dear Lee Liaison,

I have completed your online vendor registration and am writing to provide you additional information on my company and our products and services. Attached is a document providing that information.

I would like to schedule a meeting with you to provide any additional details or information that you need and to learn more about the specific requirements of your company.

Would you be available anytime during the weeks of April 10- 21?

Thank you for your time and consideration,

Vic Vendor

Your Business Name

> *Your email address*
> *Your phone number*
> *Your website*

If you met the Supplier Diversity or Purchasing contact at an event them remind them of that meeting in the email. For example:

Dear Lee Liaison,

It was a pleasure to meet you at the Chamber's Supplier Meet and Greet last week. I learned a lot from your comments about Supplier Diversity difficulties.

In your talk you advised vendors to complete your online vendor registration as a first step. I am writing to let you know that I have completed your online registration and to provide you additional information on my company and our products and services. Attached is a document providing that information.

I would like to schedule a meeting with you to provide any additional details or information that you need and to learn more about the specific requirements of your company.

Would you be available anytime during the weeks of April 10- 21?

Thank you for your time and consideration,

Vic Vendor

Your Business Name
Your email address
Your phone number
Your website

When you do meet with a Supplier Diversity contact try to identify the appropriate buyer for your products/services and obtain their contact information. Then take the next Action listed above – contact the buyer so you can establish a relationship.

The reasons for this contact are

- To provide them additional information on your company, products and services and diversity classification. This is the place to use your one-pager detailed on page 56.
- To learn their buying criteria, process and time-frames.
- To discover if there are existing contracts or other commitments that will prevent them from buying from your business and/or determine when they might be interested in your products and services.
- To begin establishing a relationship with the company's buyers and users.

Following is a form that will help you plan your contact to the Supplier Diversity contact and appropriate Buyer.

Business/ Corporation	Date to email Supplier Diversity contact	Date to meet with Supplier Diversity contact	Date to contact Buyer	Date to meet with Buyer

Keep in mind that it may take several tries to get a meeting or at least a phone conversation with the Supplier Diversity contact and/or appropriate Buyer. Sometimes these folks actually consider your persistence as a measure of your interest and professionalism. You may have to expand the above form to include additional contact attempts.

Be sure that once you have contacted a Prospect you incorporate them into your Follow Up schedule explained on page 173.

Action #76

<u>Prioritize the list of business/corporate Prospects in your profitable geographic area.</u>

In order to prioritize a list of Prospects you must establish criteria or at least some guidelines. You then must conduct research to gather information on the business/corporation and fit it into your criteria/guidelines.

The criteria/guidelines for your prioritization is unique to your business, just as any personal decision is unique to you. Some things to consider about the business/corporation when creating your prioritization criteria/guidelines are:

- Likelihood of its need/use your products or services
- Its economic stability – filed for bankruptcy, profitable, in a depressed line of business, etc.
- In a change or growth mode
- Commitment to Supplier Diversity
- Overall reputation for dealing with vendors
- Level of confidentiality and privacy

Some additional things to consider include:

- Your knowledge about the business/corporation before doing any research
- Whether you have existing contacts at the business/corporation

- Access to staff of the business/corporation through organizations, community, etc.
- Proximity to your location, cost of travel to their location

When you have created your prioritized list of Prospects plug it into the form in the following Action.

Action #77

Establish a schedule for contacting all the business/corporate Prospects in your profitable geographic area.

Use the prioritized list of Prospects from the previous Action and establish a schedule for contacting them. Use the same form on page 137 that you used for your first five business/corporate Prospects.

Remember that a schedule should be flexible enough to allow alterations when new information or circumstances make change necessary or advantageous. Use the criteria and guideline suggestions in the previous Action to help you understand what you should be looking at to help you adjust your schedule appropriately. It is advisable to use a simple spread sheet to establish your schedule so that it is easy to change dates and sort by date or Prospect.

Be sure that once you have contacted a Prospect you incorporate them into your Follow Up procedure explained on page 173.

Action #78

Make your Customers/Clients your advocates.

Word-of-Mouth is still one of the very best marketing methods. A satisfied Customer/Client will want to recommend you, vouch for you or pass your information on to someone else. It not only makes them look wise for choosing your business, it also provides them an opportunity to help a colleague, customer or client.

Doing a good job, with good being measured by the Customer/Client, is a nice advertisement. Doing an exceptional job is an excellent advertisement.

You can facilitate your Customers and Clients being advocates for your business by doing the following:

- Meet or exceed their expectations
- Use them as references*
- Use them in a press release (that you signed a new client, completed a project, helped them get a grant, developed a website for them, etc.)*
- Ask them for a letter of reference
- Mention them in your newsletter*
- Briefly describe what you did for them on your website*
- Ask them to arrange for you to speak at their professional or peer organization
- Ask them to help you present at a conference or meeting with you to describe the problem/need and the solution. (If it is a conference of their peers they will likely have to make the request or sign up to present.)
- Provide them business cards, your one-pager (see page 56) or brochures
- Give them something with your business name, logo, etc. (promotional item) that is unique and conveys something about your business. (Preferably give them something that they will use and/or display. For example: If you do training provide them a certificate of completion that is already framed and ready to hang.)

* Be sure you get their permission first!

Action #79

Plant and tend a Lead Garden.

If you want your efforts to result in revenue generating leads you need to approach it as you would a garden.

Soil: Choose your soil wisely so that you produce the leads you want. If you planted your garden in sand you would only be able to grow cactus; in red clay you might get only kudzu vines. You need soil that is receptive to your products and services. Be sure the places, organizations and websites you spend your time on are interested in your products and services.

Planting: Your seeds or seedlings need to be planted in a way that will facilitate them "taking hold." If you throw your seeds by the handfuls into your garden, very few will work their way down into the soil and actually produce a plant. Scattering your business cards, brochures, materials or time randomly will not plant your business in the minds of very many actual purchasers and users.

Fertilizing: No fertilizer may starve your garden, too much or the wrong type will kill it. Finesse will guide you in how much stimulant to apply to the marketing seeds you have planted.

Tending: A few seeds will fully mature and produce results all on their own. More will produce results if the garden is watered and weeds are cleared. Watering equates to your paying daily attention to marketing. Weeding your Lead Garden means that you clear it of things that eat up your time, effort and money and produce no revenue. Some things that can be weeds or revenue producing plants are: lead generation or networking organizations, advertising, blogging, interacting on social media sites, cold calling, media coverage, and training. Properly tending your garden means that you look closely at the plants and determine what is a weed and what will produce revenue.

Harvesting: Unfortunately produce from a garden will not fall from the plant and march itself into your kitchen. Neither will sales, contracts and projects fall into your basket. You must watch leads closely, determine when they are ripe and close the deal. Having a pretty garden is fine for flowers, but not for produce. Planting marketing seeds and generating leads are important, but be careful you don't spend all your time generating leads and rarely reap any benefits.

Replant: Most plants do not produce more than one season. Even fruit trees have to eventually be replaced. It takes replanting to continue to have revenue to harvest.

Chapter 6
<u>TRADE FAIRS & NETWORKING</u>

Action #80

<u>Incorporate the trade fair/expo basic rules into your participation in any event.</u>

Below are some very important basic rules for participating in any trade fair, vendor expo, reverse trade fair or networking event.

- Prepare (advice for the various types of events is provided in the additional Actions in this Chapter).
- Dress professionally (no jeans, no tennis shoes, dress appropriately for the products and services you offer).
- Arrive on time or a few minutes early (if you have to set up a booth then allow time for emergencies or problems such as confusion about your booth assignment or a long registration line).
- Have notebook/paper or pen for taking notes.
- Do not sit or stand behind the table in your booth.
- Smile!
- Try not to leave your booth unattended (make friends with someone in a booth nearby so that if you are alone and must leave your neighbor can watch out for your booth, offer to do the same for them).
- Have a large supply of business cards handy, such as in your pocket so you do not have to dig one out of a purse or notebook.

- Have a place to put the business cards of others – a bowl/basket in your booth, a pocket (separate from the one holding your cards).

- Be sure you have a place/folder/container to store and securely bring home all the information and materials you receive.
- Smile, look approachable, but do not be pushy.
- Say nice things and make people comfortable. Compliment them on their shirt/blouse, notice the city or agency they are from, ask them a question; remember they may be uncomfortable in a networking or trade fair situation.
- Have fun and, oh yeah, smile.

Actions #81 & #82

The following two Actions are strongly inter-linked.

<u>Identify Reverse Trade Fairs and Matchmaking/Networking Events in your profitable geographic area</u>

<u>Develop a process to prepare for Reverse Trade Fairs and Matchmaking/Networking Events</u>

Government Agencies and Supplier Diversity Organizations hold Reverse Trade Fairs and Matchmaking/Networking Events to connect purchasers and/or Prime Contractors with vendors/suppliers.

❑ A Reverse Trade Fair is an event where the purchasers and Prime Contractors have the booths. Vendors are able to talk with the purchasers; obtain materials about the things they purchase and their process; learn about their vendor requirements; find out if they need Small, Woman/Minority/ Veteran Owned or Disadvantaged Businesses; determine if they require certifications; and <u>start</u> a relationship. Some examples of these events:

- o A State purchasing/procurement department will host a fair and the various state agencies and state supported schools will have booths. Prime Contractors or major corporations in the State may also have booths. The vendors and potential vendors can visit the booths to talk with Prospects.
- o Organizations funded by SBA (Small Business Administration) such as SBDCs (Small Business Development Centers) or SCORE host regional Reverse Trade Fairs. The booths are normally allocated to state and federal agencies and their Prime Contractors – all of these are looking for Small, Minority/Woman Owned, Disadvantaged and sometimes Veteran Owned Businesses. These events often include workshops, panel discussions and real-time bid opportunities.
- o Some federal agencies or sub-agencies hold annual Reverse Trade Fairs. These events may be regional or national. The armed forces branches are one example; sometimes a specific military base or several bases in a state will hold an event that will include the base purchasers and their Prime Contractors.

❑ Matchmaking or Networking Events are opportunities for vendors to meet with purchasers and to do much the same as they can at a Reverse Trade Fair, but in a less structured setting. Sometimes these events are simply receptions. Sometimes they give you an opportunity to meet one-on-one with a specific business, government agency or education institution; these one-on-one meetings usually last fifteen to thirty minutes. Some examples of organizations that host or put on these events are:

- o Chambers of Commerce
- o Networking organizations

o Organizations specific to Woman, Minority or Veteran Ownership such as: the regional groups of NMSDC (National Minority Supplier Development Council), regional groups of WBENC (Women's Business Enterprise National Council) and the Veteran's Administration.

These are excellent opportunities, but are one step in the overall marketing course of action. It is extremely important to prepare properly for these events in order to maximize the benefit of participation. Not participating is like not showing up for the ballgame – you forfeit or, realistically, you lose without competing. Not preparing is like not bringing your bat and glove – if someone throws the ball (gives you a chance) you can't do anything with it.

Here are the suggested efforts to help you be prepared.

- Register early for the event. Put it on your calendar and don't take it off. Put time for preparation on your calendar. Put time on your calendar after the event for follow up.
- Have enough business cards with proper information
- Have a "one-pager" description of your products and services. Purchasers like one page of vital information more than they like pretty brochures. You can still give them brochures, but the "one-pager" is what they will likely keep. You may be able to make your "one-pager" into a brochure. (Action on page 56 helps you prepare a one-pager)
- Be sure that your business card, one-pager and any other materials you give out have your Woman/Minority/Veteran Owned or Disadvantaged Business Certifications listed.
- Know who will be at the event. This can be found by:
  o Looking at the promotional information about the event
  o Look at the list of past attendees. If not included in the promotional information it may be on the website. You can also ask the hosting agency, business or organization.

- o Quiz other businesses who have attended in the past
- o Look at the membership of the hosting and sponsoring organizations; they may not all attend, but at least you'll have an idea of possible attendees.
- Choose 10 of the purchaser participants that you would like to talk with. These 10 should be chosen based on your profitable geographic area (See Action on page 55). This does not mean you cannot talk with others, but if you do not choose some, you will end up wandering around and accomplishing little. If the event offers the one-on-one appointments, schedule those early or you may not get meetings with the ones you want.

- Determine what you need to know from your chosen 10 to move forward in your attempt to sell your products/services to them. You should check their website to see if there is a list of the things they purchase. If your product/service is on the list then use the event opportunity to clarify the specifics about that product/service, ask if they have a current provider and, if so, when the contract will expire. If your product/service is not on the list, but you think they could use it, then be prepared to ask. If their website tells what they expect of a vendor and you're not sure if something applies to you, then use this opportunity to find out. If they have a vendor registration form online complete it before the event. Two very important questions are:
  - o Who determines the specifications for the purchase of the products/services you provide
  - o Who makes the decision or what is the decision process for the purchase of the products/services you provide
- If the event includes workshops or speeches, determine which ones can benefit you and register for them (if required).
- If possible find out what other Small, Disadvantaged or Woman/Minority/Veteran Owned Businesses will likely attend. You may be able to find this out by talking with the

sponsoring business, agency or organization or from past attendees. This is important because it gives you an opportunity to be prepared to:

- o Scope out the competition
- o Search for possible partners
- o Find other Prospects

Note: Many of my clients have found Customer/Client among the vendor attendees at these events even if they did not get any business from the purchaser attendees.

- Dress appropriately. Business attire is normally the proper dress for these events. If you normally wear a polo shirt with your company logo, that's probably fine, since some of the purchaser attendees may be wearing something similar. Never wear jeans, dirty tennis shoes, a backpack or anything that looks as if you are on vacation. Wear something with pockets so you can use them to store your own business cards and the ones you get from others.
- Take a notebook, paper and pen for taking notes. Have a notebook or folder for storing the information you will get.

Use the following chart to help you find Events and develop a process to participate:

Task	Target Date	Actual Date	Results
Conduct research and identify Reverse Trade Fairs and Matchmaking/Network Events in your profitable geographic area			
Develop your own database of Events that you would like to participate in. *Following*			

Task	Target Date	Actual Date	Results
this chart is a basic form that you can use to gather the information. You can use paper or electronic form, which ever one you will actually use.			
Establish a preparation schedule that enables you to properly prepare for and participate in each event you have decided is "worth it". *Be sure to build in some extra time so other tasks and emergencies do not derail your plans.*			
Be sure your business cards have the proper information.			
Be sure your "one-pager" is prepared and contains all the proper information.			
Be sure your Certification, license, insurance/bonding and other information is documented on information you will provide at the Events.			
Develop a schedule to do the research to find out			

Task	Target Date	Actual Date	Results
who is likely to attend the events you plan to attend.			
Develop a schedule to do the necessary pre-event research, choose your top 10 purchaser participants for each event and determine the information you need to obtain from them.			
Decide which workshops, panel discussions, etc. you will participate in at each of your identified events. Look at the schedules for each so that you maximize the opportunities to gain information. Some topics may be repeated so look at all of the planned activities to be sure you take advantage of all that is offered.			

Suggested Basic Event Information Form

Reverse Trade Fair or Matchmaking Event
Information Form

Event Name & Type _____

Event Sponsor/Host _____

Event Date _____ Event Place _____

Who will/may attend _____

_____

_____

_____

Learning Opportunities (Workshops, etc.) _____

_____

_____

_____

Comments from past attendees _____

_____

_____

_____

Evaluators:

Will my competition be there? Y or N

Will real Prospects be there? Y or N

Are there opportunities to learn? Y or N

What is the cost? Include participation fee, cost of materials, travel cost, your hourly cost to participate (estimate number of hours to prepare and participate and multiply times your hourly rate)

_____

Other notes: _____

_____

_____

_____

Actions #83 & #84

The following two Actions are inter-dependent.

Find out if your State Government hosts a vendor expo or trade fair and evaluate the benefits of participating.

Prepare to participate in your State's vendor expo.

Most state governments host opportunities for their purchasers to meet vendors and suppliers. The event may allow vendors and suppliers to have booths. Some states use "reverse trade fairs" where the government purchasers have the booths and the vendors and suppliers can visit the ones they think are Prospects (see previous Action in this chapter starting on page 148 for preparation guidance). Some states hold events just for Woman/Minority Owned Businesses and other Disadvantaged Businesses, but some open the events up to any Small Business or even to any vendor/supplier.

In evaluating the benefits and deciding on whether to participate, be sure to include the cost and effort of preparation and follow up time. These events can offer a good opportunity to start or nurture a relationship with a Purchaser or User, but only if you have done the research to identify and qualify and if you follow up to develop the possibilities. Remember that you will be competing with other vendors/suppliers for the person's time so you need to be ready to say more than, "Hello, my name is Sandy Supplier."

One of the keys to really using this type of opportunity effectively is to identify Prospects before the event. Pick at least five state agencies, departments, offices or schools that are likely to use your products/services. Many times larger cities, counties and school districts will have representatives at these events. If you have a booth then it is a good idea to let the purchasing/procurement office or person of your best Prospects know that you will have a booth at the event and invite them to stop by. An email is the best and least expensive way to communicate with these folks. If you cannot get an email address try using a post card. The effort to identify and notify the Prospects will take some time, but it will increase your chances of making contact with real potential Clients/Customers instead of just having a lot of people take your giveaways or register for your door prize.

The following list helps you prepare for the event.

Task	Target Date	Actual Date	Results
Determine if your state or region holds a vendor expo or trade fair. Get the pertinent facts such as date, place, cost, etc.			
Evaluate the benefit and cost of participating.			
Establish a preparation schedule that enables you to properly prepare for			

Task	Target Date	Actual Date	Results
and participate in the event. *Be sure to build in some extra time so other tasks and emergencies do not derail your plans.*			
Prepare materials, purchase giveaways/promotional items.			
Determine likely Prospects and identify the best contact person(s).			
Develop email text and/or post card to send to the most likely Prospects to inform them that you will be at the event and invite them to stop by your booth.			
Send the email or post card announcement informing them that you will be at the vendor expo or trade fair.			

On the following pages is a form to help you evaluate an event and determine if the benefit of participating outweighs the cost.

State Vendor Expo, Trade Fair or Networking Event Information Form

Event Name & Type _____

Event Sponsor/Host _____

Event Date _____ Event Place _____

Frequency of Event (annual, quarterly, etc.) _____

Who will/may attend _____

_____

_____

_____

Learning Opportunities (Workshops, demonstrations, panel, etc.)

_____

_____

_____

Networking opportunities (Vendor reception or networking session, describe method, amount of time, circumstances, competition [percentage of vendors compared to purchasers, refreshments*, music*])

_____

_____

_____

_____

Comments from past attendees _____

_____

_____

Evaluators:

Will my competition be there? Y or N

Will real Prospects be there? Y or N

Are there opportunities to learn? Y or N

What is the cost? Include participation fee, cost of materials, travel cost, your hourly cost to participate (estimate number of hours to prepare and participate and multiply times your hourly rate)

_____

Other notes: _____

_____

_____

_____

---

* Most events include refreshments in vendor areas and networking events. This is thought to bring and keep people in the area. Even though this is true, some people may hide behind the selection and eating of food. You may have to make extra effort to compete by reaching out or by having something scrumptious, fun or unusual in your booth. Music is often provided in the vendor or networking area because it is thought to enhance the event. This may mean you must compete with the sound when you are talking; be sure to speak distinctly, put your materials in their hands and make use of non-verbals such as smiles, handshakes and an open stance.

Action #85

<u>Find out if there is a vendor/supplier event near you that includes Federal Agencies and their Prime Contractors; evaluate the benefits of participating.</u>

Events that provide opportunities for M/WBEs and Disadvantaged Businesses to meet representatives from Federal Agencies and their Prime Contractors are sponsored by such organizations as:

- SBDC (Small Business Development Centers)
- SBA (Small Business Administration)
- Departments of Commerce
- Chambers of Commerce
- Congressional Offices
- Women's or Minorities' Business Centers
- WBENC (Women's Business Enterprise National Council, www.wbenc.org)*
- NAWBO (National Women's Business Organization, www.nawbo.org)*
- NMSDC (National Minority Supplier Development Council, www.nmsdc.org)*
- Prime Contractors (not just construction)
- Private businesses and organizations

*These organizations are private and may be limited to members or there may be a higher participation fee for non-members. There are local/regional chapters of these organizations that may sponsor events in their specific area.

On the following pages is a form to help you evaluate an event and determine if the benefit of participating outweighs the cost.

Federal Agency or Prime Contractor
Vendor Expo, Trade Fair or Networking Event
Information Form

Event Name & Type _____

Event Sponsor/Host _____

Event Date _____ Event Place _____

Frequency of Event (annual, quarterly, etc.) _____

Who is supposed to attend _____

_____

_____

_____

_____

Does the Sponsor/Host have the ability to bring the proper
purchasers to the event? Why?

_____

_____

_____

What does the Sponsor/Host website say about past events?
(Participation, testimonies, programs, events, etc.)

_____

_____

_____

_____

Learning Opportunities (Workshops, demonstrations, panel, etc.)

_____

_____

_____

Networking opportunities (Vendor reception or networking session, describe method, amount of time, circumstances, competition, percentage of vendors compared to purchasers)

_____

_____

_____

_____

Comments from past attendees _____

_____

_____

_____

Evaluators:

Will my competition be there? Y or N

Will real Prospects be there? Y or N

Are there opportunities to learn? Y or N

What is the cost? Include participation fee, cost of materials, travel cost, your hourly cost to participate (estimate number of hours to prepare and participate and multiply times your hourly rate)

_____

Other notes: -

_____

_____

_____

Action #86

Choose a vendor/supplier event near you that includes Federal Agencies and their Prime Contractors and prepare to participate.

Using the evaluation tool in the previous Action, choose an event to participate in. Sometimes these events cover a large geographical area so you may have to travel outside your profitable geographic area to participate.

Once you have decided to participate in the event, the specifics of the event will dictate how you participate and, therefore, how you prepare. For example: If the event is a networking reception you will not do the prep steps to have a booth. As a matter of fact it is even more important for this type of event to know who will be there and decide who you want to target. That is because you will have to seek them out since you will not have a stationery site for them to drop by.

The guides in the previous Actions of this Chapter can provide preparation assistance to you if the event is a Reverse Trade Fair or Vendor/Supplier Expo.

Action #87

Be sure that you spend your Networking time with Prospects, Clients and Customers

It is so enticing to believe the promises and claims made by organizations, people and websites that invite you to join and participate. When you are promised exposure to large numbers of people, direct access to hundreds of buyers, speed-dating type contact with purchasers and almost certain sales it seems you would be foolish not to join, attend or participate.

Networking organizations (including Chambers of Commerce) and social networking websites both offer chances to reach people. You will need to evaluate any and all of these organizations in light of your business Marketing Plan.

But before you spend your time or money use the following short test to be sure you are getting the appropriate access to real prospects.

QUESTION	YES or NO	NOTES
Is this website/organization specifically for my type of Prospects, Customers, or Clients?		If yes, go to next question. If no, determine what you will get out of participating and decide if it is worth it?
Do any of my Prospects, Customers or Clients participate in this website/organization?		If yes, go to next question. If no, determine if you can learn something that will help you get access or sell to your Prospects, Customers or Clients.
Can I get access to the buyers and/or users of my Prospects, Customers or Clients?		If yes, go to next question. If no, find out who you can get access to and determine if there is a benefit.
Is there an opportunity to share information about my products and services in a		If yes, great – take advantage. If no, determine what kind of

QUESTION	YES or NO	NOTES
way that will actually reach the buyers and/or users of my Prospects, Customers or Clients?		benefit you can realize from the access to the buyers and/or users of your Prospects, Customers or Clients and what you will have to do to realize that benefit. Either way move on to the next question.
Do I (or someone on my staff) have the time, money and persistence to do what it will take to get results?		If yes, go to next question. If no, determine if there is any consequence to not participating and, if there is, rethink this question.
Is there a fee to participate?		If yes, is it worth it and is there any way I can get equal benefit with no or a lesser fee? If there is no fee, be sure you look at everything closely to be sure there is no hidden cost.
Is there enough benefit for me to spend my valuable time and money participating?		If yes, do it. If no, put on your calendar to re-evaluate in 3 to 6 months.

Action #88

Identify and evaluate participation in conferences and events of the professional organizations of your Prospects.

If there is a professional organization that your Prospects participate in then you should discover if the organization holds a conference or event that would give you access to their membership. More information on identifying and monitoring professional organizations is provided on page 94 of this book.

Following is a form to help you evaluate an event and determine if the benefit of participating outweighs the cost.

**Professional Organization Event/Meeting
Information Form**

Professional
Organization_____

Event Name & Type _____

Event Date _____ Event Place _____

Frequency of Event (annual, quarterly, etc.) _____

Who is supposed to attend _____

_____

_____

_____

_____

What is the normal/average attendance at this event

_____

_____

_____

_____

What does the Organization's website/publications say about past events? (Participation, testimonies, programs, events, etc.)

_____

_____

_____

_____

_____

What are the opportunities to participate (vendor booth, speak, sponsorship)

Participation Opportunity	Costs (include fees, travel, materials, your time, etc.)	Benefits
Vendor Booth		
Speak/ Present		
Sponsorship		
Learning (workshops, demos, panels, etc.		
Networking		
Other:_____		

Comments from past attendees _____

_____

_____

_____

Will my competition be there? Y or N

Will real Prospects be there? Y or N

Other notes: -

_____

_____

_____

_____

Action #89

<u>If you take the time and make the effort to go to an event be sure you *participate* and don't just *attend.*</u>

Participation means:

- You know the purpose of the event and can use it effectively
- You have some objectives in mind and have developed actions to accomplish them
- You take the planned actions
- You identify people, agencies, companies that you want to talk with and determine what you would like to accomplish with them
- You talk with the people, agencies, companies you identified or at least make a significant attempt

- You come away with information, contacts, clarification, future actions
- You have a follow up process and you follow that process in a timely manner

Attendance means:

- You showed up
- You introduced yourself to a few people
- You recited your "elevator speech" to some people
- You gave out some business cards to "somebody"
- You got some business cards and some information because "somebody" handed them to you
- You consider the event a success because they had great pastries
- You have no plan for further action

Action #90

Find out what works for others and adapt it for your own use.

Learning from other people's successes and mistakes is a very beneficial research tool. The benefits are compounded when determining the best participation methods for trade shows, vendor fairs and networking events because they are so time consuming and can be costly.

Here are some simple ways and places that you can conduct this research:

- Observe at the trade shows, vendor fairs and networking events. Specifically look at the following:
    o Who has steady and/or large amounts of traffic at their booth at a trade show or vendor fair.
    o Which vendors have people linger and take their material versus which vendors have people just stop to pick up the great candy or get their door prize qualification form stamped.

- o Which attendees at a Reverse Trade Fair are wandering and which ones seem to have a plan. Try to talk with the ones who seem to have a plan and find out about that plan.
- o At a network event try to determine who is talking with their friends and who is "working the room". Then watch what the room worker does and how they do it.
- Read articles, but do so with discernment. Most articles (magazines, newspapers, blogs, websites, ezines, etc.) will give you some tips or pointers, but use these suggestions to get the best:
  - o Notice the author or website and see if they have reasons to give specific advices. (Do they sell booth display equipment/signs? Do they sponsor a membership fee driven networking organization or website?)
  - o Make note of tips and suggestions that appear in multiple articles
  - o Determine if an article or the tips and suggestions are specific to a business or product/service type and be sure they apply to you.
- Ask:
  - o Your friends
  - o Your Customers/Clients
  - o Your vendors
  - o Your organization members
  - o Successful business people that you know or think participate
- Sometimes an event will offer an orientation or training session for the vendors that plan to participate. Take advantage of this if offered because they may give you some new pointers and they will certainly tell you all the logistic and housekeeping information of that event so you can avoid problems and difficulties.
- Make notes about your successes, mistakes, disappointments, problems, etc on the events in which you

participate so you can modify your efforts next time. Do not assume you will remember something just because it was very good or very bad. Think about the times you ran up against a problem and said, "Oh yeah, I remember this from last time. How could I have forgotten." Write it down and make a file (electronic, paper or both) on each event and pull it out next time.

Action #91

Research Reverse Trade Fairs, State and Federal vendor events in other areas and evaluate participation.

Once you have evaluated and participated in events near you it is time to consider expanding your reach through events in other regions and states. However, remember that you should only participate in events that are attended by Prospects that need your products and services in your profitable geographical area. See page 55 for guidance in establishing your profitable geographical area.

Action #92

Develop a long-term plan to participate in trade fairs and vendor events.

The previous Actions of this chapter will help you establish this long-term plan. The follow up information on page 175 will help you develop the "after the events" portion of your plan.

Chapter 7
<u>FOLLOW UP / FOLLOW THROUGH</u>

Action #93

<u>Keep your reputation positive</u>.

If you do not live up to the promises and claims you make, you will lose existing Customer/Client or never really have a chance with a new Prospect. Sometimes it is easy to get caught up in the moment and say yes when you should not. Be sure that you do not let excitement and enthusiasm overrule your capabilities. Do not sign the contract unless you know you can do everything promised and required in the manner it must be done according to the specified schedule. Remember that word-of-mouth is the best or worst friend of a Small Business; if you do fall victim to over promising or committing people will know. Also, many government agencies and businesses can, and may, exclude you from future bidding and consideration if you fail to meet your commitments.

Action #94

<u>Develop a procedure for follow up</u>.

Follow up is essential to marketing and is desired and expected by Prospects, Customers and Clients. Yet, it is something that many people either do not do effectively or do not do at all. If you do not have a procedure for follow up, you will likely not do it or at least not do it consistently. Developing the procedure is making a promise to yourself and your business to increase opportunities. It will also set you apart from almost everyone else because so few people do appropriate follow up.

In doing marketing research for clients I often talk with purchasers or Supplier Diversity coordinators to find out what common mistakes vendors and suppliers make. One of the most common answers is that they do not follow up. The purchasers and coordinators tell me that would-be suppliers/vendors miss the following chances to shine:

- Sending information when requested
- Reminding a purchaser that they are still out there ready to supply
- Giving a quote when they promise to do so
- Bidding or providing a "No-Bid" response when given an opportunity

A follow-up procedure might be something like this:

- If you are attending an event or have opportunity to meet with a Prospect, put a time on your calendar to do follow up.
- Keep business cards and other information you gather in a specific place until you have done a follow up.
- Develop the text for follow up letters, emails and materials. Be sure that the materials include proper statements and information about being Small, Woman/Minority/Veteran Owned or Disadvantaged and associated Certifications.
- Use your tickler file, email reminder or similar system to nag you until you do the follow up.
- Do not take the follow up entry off your calendar and try not to postpone it.
- Once you have done the follow up move the business cards and materials to appropriate files based on expected future actions.
- Do additional follow up as needed to stay in front of the real Prospects.

The chart below provides some guidance for developing your follow up procedure.

Situation	Follow Up Activity	Time Frame
Have initial meeting with a Prospect	Send thank you email or letter and any information you promised	Within 4 days *
Meet a Prospect at a Reverse Trade Fair or Matchmaking/Networking Event	If an action was suggested to you (sending information, registering as a vendor, etc.) do it. Then send a "nice to meet you" email or letter and let them know you followed their direction.	Within a week *
Meet a potential Prospect at any event	Send a "nice to meet you" email or letter along with information about your products/services if appropriate	Within a week *
You did immediate follow up, but have not had an opportunity to bid or propose	Do a second follow up with new or additional information	3 to 6 months after initial follow up
You made initial contact but have not heard anything from the Prospect nor had an opportunity to bid or	Do additional follow ups at regular intervals; try to find something new or	3 to 6 month intervals

Situation	Follow Up Activity	Time Frame
propose	interesting to say or write (new product or service, new clients, new or revamped website, new location, new contact information, etc.)	
You have not had an order from or communication with a Client/Customer in a long-time	Do follow ups at regular intervals similar to the Activity above. You could also use the "we've missed you" approach.	Interval depends on what is logical and possible for your products/services and the Client's needs. (i.e. if your product/ service or their need is seasonal)

* Immediate follow up is fine.

Action #95

Develop a process to keep registrations current.

It is vital that you keep information on your business current in places where you have registered as a potential vendor or supplier. That includes:

- CCR (see page 106)
- Any Federal Agency that maintains its own database of potential vendors (i.e. the US Department of Veteran's Affairs http://www.vetbiz.gov/).
- Any State government purchasing or vendor database

- Any specific state agency that has its own purchasing or vendor database
- Any local government (city/county) purchasing or vendor database
- Any school district purchasing or vendor database
- Any business/corporate vendor database
- Any organization (such as Chambers, AGC [Association of General Contractors], WBENC [Women's Business Enterprise National Council], etc.) that maintains databases on Small Businesses, W/MBEs, Veteran Owned or Disadvantaged Business
- Any database where you have registered as a potential vendor/supplier.

If the information in a database is not correct you may miss an opportunity. Here is a list of common wrong information and the resulting problem.

Common Wrong Information	Resulting Problem
Old telephone number or email address	They cannot contact you
Old address	They cannot send you notices and bids
Lack of new NAICS or NIGP codes (explanation on these codes is provided on pages 11 and 12)	You get passed over when they are looking for specific identifier codes
Lack of information on new/additional products and services	They do not consider you for opportunities because they do not know you can do/provide something
Wrong contact person/information	They probably will only make one attempt

The safest practice for updating registrations is to set specific times on your calendar in 3 or 6 month intervals. However, if you make a major change it is important to update your registrations immediately.

Following is a suggested procedure:

- Determine who in your company will do the updating. This involves checking each database to see if it is current and making any necessary changes.
- Determine if it needs to be done every 3 months or every 6 months. This will be determined by how often changes occur in your business. Once a year is not often enough. (It might be helpful if you associate the updating with something that is inevitable or necessary, such as changing your clocks when Daylight Saving Time starts or ends.)
- Put the action on the calendar of the person who will do the updating. Do not remove it.
- Start a list of databases where you have registered. Be sure the list includes the name of the agency, business or organization, the website and any information you need to "log in". (Include the government agencies, schools or businesses that you have sent letters to asking to be on their vendor list. You do not need to send them a new letter unless you have made a change.)
- Every time your business registers in a new database add the appropriate information to the list.
- Remember that being on a list does not guarantee you business, but it is normally a requirement or pre-requisite.

If you use some type of customer management software or system you may be able to incorporate these individual databases into that system to help you keep them updated

Action #96

<u>Determine if a newsletter will actually help you market your products and services. If it will – implement it.</u>

If a newsletter truly induces your Prospects, Customers and Clients to purchase your products and services then it is a good marketing tool. If it does not then you may want to find a more effective tool.

Here are a few things to consider in deciding whether to start, continue or modify a newsletter:

- Do you or someone on your staff have the time to produce a quality newsletter?
- Can you afford the cost of producing a quality newsletter (hiring a professional, your time away from other tasks, subscribing to a service that provides the articles, etc.)?
- Do you or someone on your staff have the time to maintain a distribution list; or can you afford the cost to buy one?
- Are you sure the people on your self-maintained or purchased distribution list are truly Prospects, Customers or Clients?
- Are the people who can purchase your products and services reading the newsletter?
- Is the newsletter causing people to purchase your products and services?
- Is the newsletter reminding people that can purchase your products and services that you are still ready to serve?
- Is the newsletter driving people to your website?
- Based on your own personal history, if you start it will you continue it? If yes, will you continue it long enough to justify the initial investment of money and time?
- Would periodic, timely articles sent to a distribution list and/or posted on social media websites be as or more effective as a newsletter? (This would likely take less time and be more inexpensive.)

- Would you accomplish your purposes through occasional contributions to the newsletter(s) of other businesses and/or organizations?

These questions are to help you step back from the widespread claim that "businesses need to publish a newsletter" and analyze the benefits, or lack of, for your specific business.

Action #97

Use social or new media to drive people to your business or at least your website.

Books, articles, webinars, seminars, workshops and opinions abound on how Small Businesses can effectively use social medial and other forms of the "new media". There are Social Media sites and communities catering to anything and everything. If you want to post, share, present a webinar, listen to a webinar, comment, blog, watch a video, listen to an Internet radio program or host an Internet radio program you have multiple opportunities for each.

But how do you use all these interaction opportunities to make money?

Using social or new media in ways that will cause people to act in a manner that will benefit you is extremely personal to your business. The following factors should be put into the equation to determine what is a positive and what is a negative for you.

- Who are you trying to reach and how do they utilize social/new media?
- What action do you want to stimulate?
- Do you have the time to effectively use social/new media? (The more options, the more time to identify, qualify and use.)
- Can you appropriately separate business from personal in your use of social/new media?
- Will using social/new media have any negative impact?

- What are the consequences if you do not use social/new media?

If you have an actual product that can be purchased, social/new media may be more effective than if you provide a service. Social and new media are about immediacy and having a product that can be purchased instantly works well. However, if you can cause any audience to act in a way that benefits your business then it is probably a good marketing tool.

Be very careful that you don't get caught up in the fever and spend your time in social/new media activities that have no goal other than to "get your name out there." It may be helpful to modify marketing activities that already work for you into things that will fit into social/new media.

This is a good place to learn from others. Ask several people who are using social/new media what benefit they are experiencing. If they respond with something general such as "increased exposure," press them to tell you what benefit the "increased exposure" has given them. When you find someone that honestly has measurable benefits, try to apply/adapt their methods to your situation.

Action #98

<u>If one of your target Prospects has had a significant event in his/her life send them a congratulatory note.</u>

This is a good opportunity to remind them that you are still around and to show them that you pay attention to their accomplishments. If you haven't made an introductory contact to them yet, then include the congratulations in your introductory contact.

Here is a list of things that merit a congratulatory note:

- Named to a Board or Committee (especially if it is related to Supplier Diversity)
- Received an award (particularly if it is associated with Supplier Diversity)

- Received a promotion
- Celebrated a milestone work anniversary
- Had a milestone birthday
- Got married
- Had a baby

Once you start watching for things to congratulate you will notice other things. Remember that everyone likes to be complimented and recognized for accomplishments.

Action #99

Develop a system to send a card to Prospects, Customers and Clients on unusual holidays or significant days.

It is almost a given that businesses will send cards, even gifts, to their Prospects, Clients and Customers on some typical days or during major holidays. To utilize the practice of sending a card or giving a token to your best advantage do it on it at a time that other people may not be using.

Here are some ideas to stimulate ideas for sending a card or gift to celebrate an unusual day and remind your Prospect, Client or Customer that you are still around.

- Card or flowers on the first day of spring
- "Thank you for your business" card on Thanksgiving
- "Proposal" on Leap Day (February 29, which occurs every four years). *Leap Day folk tradition is that the woman can propose to a man. A Woman-Owned Business could use this Day to her advantage.*
- A hat with your logo or message on National Hat Day (January 25)
- Card with a silly poem on Bad Poetry Day (August 18)
- Card about discovery on Columbus Day (second Monday in October)

Chapter 8
<u>SCHEDULE</u>

Action #100

<u>Establish a schedule for your Marketing Plan</u>

Many of the Actions in this book advise that you list activities and set dates for doing them. Other Actions offer suggestions and examples. If you will take these Actions and plug them into a schedule with start and complete dates you will have a Marketing Plan. Of course you will need to add and tailor to suit your specific business, but this book gives you some realistic Actions that will definitely get you started.

If you already use a scheduling or project management system you can use it to develop your Marketing Plan Schedule. If you do not already have a method then you can use a simple spread sheet or table. Using a spread sheet or table allows you to adjust, edit or add easily. If you are considering purchasing a scheduling or project management system be sure that it is not so complicated or cumbersome that you will end up not using it.

Here are some ideas about how to utilize a spread sheet or table for your schedule:

- List activities in the left hand column
- Put times (specific dates, months, weeks, quarter, etc.) in the column headings

On the following pages are some illustrations:

Action/Task	1st Qtr 2010	2nd Qtr 2010	3rd Qtr 2010	4th Qtr. 2010	1st Half 2011	2nd Half 2011	2012

Action /Task	Jan	Feb	Mar	Apr	May	Jun	Jul	Aug	Sep	Oct	Nov	Dec

If your schedule gets complicated, lengthy or spreads over multiple years you may want to use some other simple tricks to keep it organized. Here are a few suggestions:

- Separate or color code by type of Action/Task
- Build in additional columns or headings to enable you to sort

- Leave blank columns or rows if you print it and post it so you can hand write notes or add stickers. (Remember that a previous Action suggested that you build in rewards for accomplishments – you can provide space in your schedule to put a gold star, a check mark or other psychological reward.)
- Build time into your schedule to do adjustments
- Transfer Actions/Tasks into your calendar and that of your staff. Do this on a regular basis to insure that tasks are completed and done on time.

Action #101

Schedule a regular and recurring time for Research.

One of the most important things you can learn from this book, is that it is essential that you do RESEARCH. Many of the Actions suggest research that will save time, improve your chances of success, set you apart from your competition or provide some other important benefit. However, most people do not like to do research or do it when they "have time". To insure that you do appropriate research, schedule time to do it on a regular basis. You will have to decide when you can do it and how much time you can spend based on your personality, the fluidity of your business and the amount of help you have. Here are some suggestions that have worked for other people:

- Dedicate one lunch-at-your desk session per week
- Come in one hour early twice a month
- Schedule one afternoon per month
- Do an intensive research session for two days each summer and the week between December 25th and 31st (These are both times when it's hard to get things done, so go exploring instead)

The most important thing is that you schedule it. Plug it into the Marketing Action Plan schedule, put it on your calendar and treat it as you would an appointment with a client – it does not get canceled or even changed except for honest-to-goodness emergencies!

Chapter 9
LIST OF ACTIONS

Here is a list of all the 101 Actions in the book and the page number they start on. You can use this list for the following purpose:

- Check off Actions as you complete them
- Make notes or set dates for using or reconsidering an Action
- Page number for quickly finding an Action

CHECK OFF OR NOTES/DATES FOR FUTURE USE	#	ACTION	PAGE #
		Chapter 1 **BEGINNING**	
	1	Learn these acronyms and words.	5
	2	Be sure your Prospects, Customers and Clients understand what your Products and Services are.	6
	3	If your objective is to help people, start or join a non-profit organization.	7
	4	Know and respect your competition.	8

	5	Accept the fact that registration with Prospects is an essential step in the marketing process, but is not the last step. Prepare yourself to register.	8
	6	Obtain a Federal Tax ID Number.	10
	7	Determine the SIC and NAICS Codes that apply to your business.	11
	8	Determine the NIGP Codes that apply to and identify your business products and services to local government agencies.	12
	9	Obtain DUNS Number.	13
	10	Determine if one or more Certifications would be advantageous to your business.	14
	11	If any Certifications will be advantageous develop a schedule for applying.	19
	12	Establish a system to reward you and/or your staff when you accomplish important Actions.	20
	13	Guard against spending too much time on "getting ready" instead of "doing" .	21
		Chapter 2 **PHILOSOPHY**	
	14	Understand the terms Supplier Diversity and Vendor Diversity and determine how they apply	25

		to your business.	
	15	Recognize that being a Small Business, Woman/Minority/Veteran Owned or a Disadvantaged Business is a *Marketing Angle* and not the foundation of your business or the basis of your marketing plan.	26
	16	Know who your customers/clients are.	28
	17	Understand that what you sell or provide is not what is important to your Prospect or customer/client.	32
	18	Recognize that relationships are the heart of buying and selling.	33
	19	Appreciate that the User of your product or service is your real target.	37
	20	Realize that you must identify and develop a relationship with the User of your products and services. Identify the User of you products and services at some of your target Prospects.	39
	21	Accept the fact that the Purchasing/ Procurement Staff are the rule keepers and they are not the User.	40
	22	Adopt the philosophy of always reading the "How to do business with" information on any	42

	30	Determine the geographic area in which you can profitably provide your products or services.	55
	31	Develop a one-pager on your company.	56
		These two Actions are listed together because they are so closely coupled.	
	32	Use an email address that has your business name after the @.	63
	33	Get a website	63
	34	Include your Minority/Woman/Veteran Owned or Disadvantaged Certifications or Small Business status on your website.	64
	35	Incorporate your Small, Disadvantaged or Minority/Woman/Veteran Owned status and marketing angle into your Marketing Plan.	65
	36	Prepare a template letter requesting to be placed on "Vendor" or "Bidder" list.	66
	37	Develop and use a customer/client Contract that includes a Scope of Work.	69
	38	Create and utilize a Non-Disclosure Agreement	73
	39	Create and use a contract with	74

	47	Take advantage of the fact that many major corporations that have Supplier Diversity Policies and/or Programs expect their major suppliers to also have policies.	90
	48	Identify professional organizations that your Prospects participate in and find ways to benefit from observing and/or participating.	94
		Chapter 5 **GETTING THE WORD OUT/** **GETTING NOTICED**	
	49	Develop, categorize and maintain an email Distribution List.	101
	50	Include your Small, Disadvantaged or Ownership status on your business cards..	102
	51	Include your Small Business status or Disadvantaged or Minority/Woman/Veteran Owned Certifications on your brochures and other marketing materials.	103
	52	Announce new Certifications to those who care.	105
	53	Register on CCR (Central Contractor Registration). If you are already registered be sure your information is current.	106

	54	Register as a Vendor with your County government	108
	55	Determine which departments or offices in your county government need your products and services.	111
	56	Make a list of the counties in the first hundred miles of your geographic circle (the geographic area you can profitably serve) and develop a schedule for registering in their database.	113
	57	Establish a schedule to complete the departmental list on each of the counties in the previous list.	114
	58	Register as a Vendor with the city where you business is located (or is near)	115
	59	Determine which department or departments in your city government need your products and services.	115
	60	Make a list of appropriate cities in the first hundred miles of your geographic circle (the geographic area you can profitably serve) and develop a schedule for registering in their database.	116
	61	Establish a schedule to complete the departmental list on each of the cities/towns in the previous list.	118

	62	Examine the utility providers in your area to see if they are likely Prospects.	119
	63	Register as a Vendor with the School District nearest your business	121
	64	Identify departments, offices and initiatives in the School Districts nearest you that are likely to use your products or services.	123
	65	Make a list of the school districts in the first hundred miles of your geographic circle (the geographic area you can profitably serve) and develop a schedule for registering in their database.	125
	66	Establish a schedule to complete the departmental list on each of the school districts in the previous list.	126
	67	Register as a vendor with your home State.	127
		Following are two Actions that work together to help you sell your products and services to State Departments of Transportation.	
	68	Register as a Vendor with your State Department of Transportation (DOT)	129
		Apply for Certification as a DBE (Disadvantaged Business	

	69	Enterprise) by your State DOT	129
	70	Register as a vendor with the state supported university or college nearest you.	131
	71	Identify and contact the appropriate departments, schools, institutions, foundations, initiatives or other entities within the university or college nearest you.	132
	72	Find out where your government and education prospects post their bidding opportunities and monitor the postings.	133
	73	Choose five of the most likely business and/or corporate Prospects for your products and services in your profitable geographic area and register in their database.	136
		The following two Actions are covered together because the second is dependent on the purpose for the first.	
	74	Once you have completed the online vendor registration for the five Prospects in your profitable geographic area contact the Supplier Diversity coordinator or the Purchasing Department.	137
		Contact the designated Buyer for your products/services at	

		the benefits of participating.	
	84	Prepare to participate in your State's vendor expo.	156
	85	Find out if there is a vendor/supplier event near you that includes Federal Agencies and their Prime Contractors; evaluate the benefits of participating.	161
	86	Choose a vendor/supplier event near you that includes Federal Agencies and their Prime Contractors and prepare to participate.	164
	87	Be sure that you spend your Networking time with Prospects, Clients and Customers	164
	88	Identify and evaluate participation in conferences, events of the professional organizations of your Prospects.	167
	89	If you take the time and make the effort to go to an event be sure you *participate* and don't just *attend*.	169
	90	Find out what works for others and adapt it for your own use.	170
	91	Research Reverse Trade Fairs, State and Federal vendor events in other areas and evaluate participation.	172

	92	Develop a long-term plan to participate in trade fairs and vendor events.	172
		Chapter 7 **FOLLOW UP / FOLLOW THROUGH**	
	93	Keep your reputation positive.	173
	94	Develop a procedure for follow up.	173
	95	Develop a process to keep registrations current.	176
	96	Determine if a newsletter will actually help you market your products and services. If it will – implement it.	179
	97	Use social or new media to drive people to your business or at least your website.	180
	98	If one of your target Prospects has had a significant event in his/her life send them a congratulatory note.	181
	99	Develop a system to send a card to Prospects, Customers and Clients on unusual holidays or significant days.	182

ABOUT THE AUTHOR

Janet W. Christy has spent the majority of her professional career in marketing, sales and public relations positions.

In 2003 Janet formed Leverage & Development, LLC, a consulting firm focused on helping Small, Disadvantaged and Woman/Minority Owned businesses and the agencies and organizations that work with them.

Janet currently works with businesses to develop plans that will help them maximize their Small, Disadvantaged or Ownership status. She prepares a customized manual for her clients that includes: Market Assessment, Key Prospects, Prospecting Strategy, and a Step-by-Step Marketing Plan.

Janet also conducts seminars on marketing and certification for Small, Disadvantaged and Woman/Minority Owned Businesses. She conducts the seminars for Chamber of Commerce memberships, private businesses, education institutions and municipal/county governments. These workshops provide attendees with practical instruction, resources and experience-based advice.

In 2006 Janet's fist book *Capitalizing On Being Woman Owned* was released. This book is still available through bookstores and online booksellers such as Amazon.com and Barnes&Noble.com. Janet has also written articles for several magazines and blogs including "Home Business Magazine." She has made more than 30 radio appearances to discuss the advantages and opportunities for Small Businesses. Janet was selected as part of the "Brain Trust" for the Small Business Advocate (www.smallbusinessadvocate.com). She was named as "Communicator of the Year" by the Greenville SC Chapter of the Association for Women in Communications. She continues to speak and conduct workshops related to Small, Women and Minority Owned Businesses.

Janet has worked on both sides of the procurement process. Her experience includes both preparing RFPs (Request for Proposal) and RFIs (Request for Information) and responding to them. She currently works as a consultant for Small and Woman/Minority Owned Businesses to aid them in marketing to government and education entities. She also assists government and education entities in the development of RFPs and the evaluation of responses. Janet's firm, Leverage & Development, LLC offers a workshop to help businesses understand the culture behind government purchasing.

Because of Janet's experience and unique grass roots research methods she is often called on by both businesses, government entities and non-profit organizations to conduct feasibility, needs assessments and other complex studies. Reports from Leverage & Development, LLC provide detailed information and practical applications that are easily adapted for business plans, operational guidelines, and grant applications.

Before becoming a Consultant and Author, Janet spent more than 25 years in the telecommunications industry. In late 1999, Janet, along with several partners, formulated, raised angel and bank financing, and implemented the business plan for a telecommunications company specializing in back-office and consulting services for Internet Service Providers (ISPs), Virtual ISPs and Competitive Local Exchange Carriers (CLECs). The group launched the telecommunications company and within less than a year sold the ISP portion to a publicly traded company. Janet served as Executive Vice President for Sales, Marketing and Customer Service.

At the website of her firm Leverage & Development, LLC www.leverageanddevelopment.com, you can find more information about Janet along with helpful articles and guides she has written. She can be contacted at janet@leverageanddevelopment.com. Janet is also the host of two other websites www.janetchristy.com and www.businesshospitalforwomen.com.

LaVergne, TN USA
19 July 2010
190032LV00004B/3/P